THE
MONASTERY GARDEN
COOKBOOK

THE MONASTERY GARDEN COOKBOOK

Farm-Fresh Recipes for the Home Cook

Brother Victor-Antoine
d'Avila-Latourrette

Cover photos by Mick Hales
Cover and interior design by Liz Trovato

Produced by Print Matters, Inc., www.printmattersinc.com

Published by The Countryman Press, P.O. Box 748, Woodstock, VT 05091
Distributed by W. W. Norton & Company, Inc., 500 Fifth Avenue, New York,
NY 10110

The Monastery Garden Cookbook
ISBN: 978–0–88150–923–6
Library of Congress CIP data have been applied for.

10 9 8 7 6 5 4 3 2 1

Printed in Canada

In loving memory of Sister Marie-Placide Deliard and Mother Stephen Prokes, whose garden skills and exemplary monastic lives inspired many, including my own daily work in our monastic gardens and kitchen.

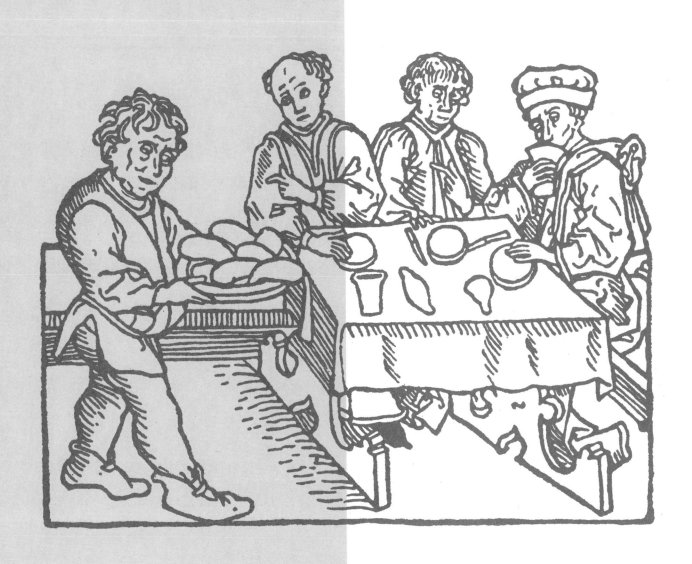

CONTENTS

This is what the Lord Almighty, the God of Israel, says . . . plant gardens and eat what they produce.

—JEREMIAH 39:5

An Easy Way to Find Your Favorite Vegetable Recipes

The Monastery Garden Cookbook not only brings to the kitchens of its readers nearly two hundred inventive ways to enhance vegetables as they are prepared for meals, but also serves as a convenient guide to the essential background of vegetables themselves. Accordingly, unlike my previous books, which were organized seasonally, this book follows an entirely new plan. Each of the vegetables in common use in North America is the focus of an independent section, with its own brief introduction emphasizing that vegetable's individuality, origin, and traditional uses in cooking. It may be surprising to see how uses have changed over the years; vegetables once considered exotic are now as common as tomatoes, which themselves were once considered exotic. The introductions will be especially helpful to those interested in trying some of the vegetables that are less familiar.

The vegetable sections are arranged in alphabetical order, for convenience. Throughout the introductions and the recipes you will find suggestions for seasonal use, so the emphasis on freshness is also very much evident. At the end of the book, as an additional aid, you will find a seasonal organization of the vegetables.

It is important to keep in mind, however, that the seasons overlap, as do the use and availability of some vegetables, especially those harvested at the tail end of their season. For example, asparagus and peas are considered essentially spring vegetables, but sometimes one continues to harvest and enjoy them throughout early summer. Likewise, harvest and availability of some summer vegetables, such as corn and tomatoes, continue throughout the fall months until a hard frost kills the plants.

All sorts of grain which our own land
    doth yield
Was hither brought, and sown in every field:
As wheat and rye, barley, oats, bean and peas
Here all thrive and they profit from them raise,
All sorts of roots and herbs in gardens grow—
Parsnips, carrots, turnips or what you'll sow,
Onions, melons, cucumbers, radishes,
Skirets, beets, coleworts and fair cabbages.

—WILLIAM BRADFORD

INTRODUCTION

A few years ago, a fine young student who occasionally liked to visit our small monastery went off to France. While there, he decided to see some of the many monasteries across the French landscape. Upon his return to this country, I asked him what he had discovered that had most impressed him in the places he had visited. Without hesitation, the young man exclaimed, "Ah, the gardens of the monasteries, those gardens lovingly tended by the monks."

At first, I was surprised at his response. I had expected him to mention perhaps the beauty of the monastic churches or the unforgettable music of the chants in the Offices, for example. Of course, he found the prayerful Offices to be a deeply spiritual experience, he said, but he was most enchanted by what he found in the monastic gardens.

"There is real life in those gardens," he went on, "and one can almost feel the pulse of a particular monastic community by the work that is being accomplished there in the gardens." He recalled for me how the charming and brightly colored miniatures from the ancient monastic manuscripts, where we often see a monk or nun depicted at work in the garden, suddenly became alive for him and deeply expressive of meaning.

In all our monasteries, of course, the occupation of gardening is as old as monastic life itself. Gardens and the constant tending of them have always been an integral part of our tradition. The first monks went about elaborating the principles of monastic gardening in the deserts of Egypt and Palestine, in the same way and at the same time that they elaborated the first rules and principles that were to become the base of their monastic living. For example, we read in an early life of Saint Antony, the first monk and the father of all monks, an episode that relates to his work in the garden: "These vines and these little trees did he plant; the pool did he contrive, with much labor for the watering of his garden; with his rake did he break up the earth for many years."

It is obvious from this description that Saint Antony worked very hard in his garden, and that the main reason for cultivating it was to provide food for himself and other monks, as well as for the poor and the pilgrims that came to see him. Saint Antony took to heart the biblical counsel that one must eat from the labor of one's hands. Two centuries later, Saint Benedict would insist on the importance of the same teaching by stating in his Rule that "they are truly monks when they live by the labor of their hands, as did our fathers and the Apostles." That meant for Saint Benedict that the monks had to work long hours in their gardens, orchards, and mills, producing the food necessary for the monastic table. And since the monastic regimen tends to be almost exclusively vegetarian, the cultivation of vegetable gardens and the care and maintenance of vineyards and orchards became of primary importance in the life of all monasteries. In this context, we can understand how some monks became passionate gardeners down through the centuries. There is, for example, the eighth-century monk Walafrid Strabo of the Abbey of Reichenau, who went so far as to praise gardening in a work called *De cultura hortorum* (*On the Cultivation of Gardens*).

It was not only the monks who devoted time and skills in great measure to the work and the art of gardening. The nuns, living under the same Rule of Saint Benedict, invested their unique talents in this work, as we see from the case of the twelfth-century abbess Saint Hildegard of Bingen. Her combined knowledge of agriculture and medicine inspired her to write two treatises on the nutritional and medicinal qualities of the various plants, herbs, and vegetables that her nuns cultivated in the monastery gardens. Saint Hildegard strongly recommended that the vegetables prepared in the kitchen be fresh and recently harvested in order to retain their vital energies and obtain all nutritional benefits. Saint Hildegard insisted on the principle that as human beings we exist not in isolation but always in a mutually dependent relationship with the whole universe. Thus, it was extremely important to her that people should learn to live harmoniously with the rhythm of the seasons, and this was to include a diet based on the fresh vegetables and fruits harvested from the gardens and orchards of the monastery. She firmly believed in what we would today call an "organic-biological process" that respects the rhythm of the seasons, the inner cohesion of all creation, and the natural laws that help maintain order and balance in the universe. By living thus, Saint Hildegard believed, human beings can achieve balance and health in their own personal lives.

History has shown that monks and nuns have always been vigilant stewards and avid cultivators of the land entrusted to them. The time allotted to them each year for full- or part-time gardening, from the moment of planting the first seed to the moment the last vegetable is harvested, is a rewarding and, indeed, an intense time of joy. This is so in spite of the hard and never-ending nature of the work. Of course, the real reward is felt when the fresh new vegetables begin to be served at the monastic table, delighting all who partake. Gardening is both a task and an art. The solid experience accumulated over many years brings the gardener mastery of the proper methods and many intricate secrets necessary to achieve reliable success. Nothing, indeed, can take the place of that experience. The gardener must be sensitively attuned to the growing seasons, to the local weather, to the quality of the soil, and so forth . . . and always allow Mother Nature to be the guide.

Each season has its own significance. There is a time to prepare and build the soil, a time for planting and germination, a time for cultivation and growth, and a time for yielding fruit and harvesting. Each season, too, provides its own variety of vegetables—some for spring and summer, some for fall and even winter. Living and gardening in tune with the seasons permits the monk or nun gardener to provide for the table vegetables rich with vitamins and nutrients, wonderful with the taste of freshness, and beautiful in exquisite colors and textures. The vegetables thus harvested are brought to the monastery kitchen, where they are treated with great respect. It remains for the cook to use talent and taste to create imaginative dishes that can be savored and remembered by the monastic palate long after the food has been consumed.

Of course, not everyone has a plot of land or the time to cultivate a garden, infinitely desirable as this may be. However, in the present day and age, that is not a good reason for passing up fresh vegetables. Today we have enviably wide opportunities to find fresh vegetables at supermarkets throughout the land, as well as at farmers' markets, at roadside stands, and in a variety of other ways in cities and in the country. Freshness makes all the difference in the world. Any cook concerned about solid nutrition and wonderful flavors will seek out the freshest possible vegetables to be found locally. Fresh vegetables retain most of their nutritional value and provide a standard of texture and taste that is excellence itself.

The recipes in this book do not include meat. This does not mean that they are designed for the vegetarian alone. Vegetables are for everyone! In creating and presenting these new recipes to the public, it never entered my mind that they were to be used by only one group of people. On the contrary, these recipes were created, first, for each and every person who is interested in a healthy diet; and second, for all those who are tired of presenting vegetables at the table in the same old way and are looking for good, innovative recipes that reflect the boundless opportunities that vegetables present. While many of these recipes are self-sufficient as they are, the majority also go well with meat, egg, and fish dishes. Some may be used to create wonderful soups or appetizers, others for salads, and still others as either a main dish or an accompaniment to a main dish. It will be up to the imagination of the chef to adapt or re-create these recipes as a surprise for family and guests. My most ardent hope is that vegetables will be rediscovered in a new light, be in demand more than ever before, and, most of all, become the essential foundation of a cuisine that will be both healthier and more refined.

Finally, I wish to use this introduction as an opportunity to thank all those dear friends here in the United States and in France who encouraged me and supported me during the long, sometimes burdensome, but always rewarding task of preparing this book. I wish to thank all those who closely collaborated in bringing out this new book: Kermit Hummel and Lisa Sacks of The Countryman Press; my producer Richard Rothschild at Print Matters; Jennifer Lyons of the Jennifer Lyons Literacy Agency; Liz Trovato, whose elegant design made the recipes more enticing and accessible; Kathy Herald Marlowe and Michael Marlowe for the generous use of their beautiful kitchen. Michael Centore, who patiently worked on many of the book's details; and the student interns from Vassar College who helped at the monastery and with typing and a great many other tasks. My sincere gratitude to all. I hope these recipes help enhance la bonne table in your home and bring joy to you, your family, and your friends.

ARTICHOKES

(Cynara scolymus)

Like many other vegetable species that have survived to our day, the artichoke had its origins in the countries surrounding the Mediterranean Sea. In ancient Greek literature, there are frequent references to the artichoke. The Egyptians, besides eating them, also consumed the boiled salted water in which they were cooked, as a medicine for certain ailments. The Romans often used the artichoke as an accompaniment to their most gourmet dishes, frequently serving it with their finest fish dishes. It was through the Romans that the artichoke was introduced into Spain and France and later to other areas of Europe. A bit forgotten by the aristocracy during the Middle Ages, the artichoke was rediscovered and revived during the Renaissance, first by a certain Filippo Strozzi in Florence around 1466, and later in France by Catherine de Médicis, for whom the artichoke was a favorite vegetable—indeed, she considered it a delicacy. During her reign, she expanded its cultivation throughout France. By the time of King Henry IV, the artichoke was not only eaten routinely in the cities and countryside of France, it was also used as an aphrodisiac. From France, Spain, and Italy, the cultivation of the artichoke expanded, especially early in the 20th century, to other countries with mild climates, such as Argentina, and to certain areas of the United States, especially California.

The artichoke today is an integral part of certain refined cuisines, especially those that come to us from France, Spain, Italy, Greece, and other places. It is often used in salads, served as an appetizer, and added to dishes such as risotto and pasta as one of the main ingredients. The artichoke contains vitamins A, B, and C, which makes it a desirable vegetable from a health point of view.

It takes a certain amount of practice and patience to cook fresh artichokes, which is why when pressed for time, the reluctant cook should not hesitate to use frozen or even canned artichokes in ordinary or everyday cooking.

ARTICHOKES BASQUE STYLE

This dish makes a wonderful appetizer any time of the year.

4 artichokes, trimmed
4 tablespoons lemon juice
1 small head leaf lettuce
4 medium tomatoes, sliced in quarters
4 hard-boiled eggs, sliced in rounds
1 small red onion, thinly sliced
green olives

Vinaigrette
7 tablespoons olive oil
2 tablespoons wine vinegar
2 tablespoons lemon juice
salt and freshly ground pepper to taste

1. Cook the artichokes in salted water mixed with the 4 tablespoons of lemon juice for 30 minutes until the artichokes become tender. Remove them from the heat and rinse them in cold water. Separate and discard the leaves; remove the artichoke hearts, put them in a covered container, and chill them until ready to use.

2. Just before you are ready to serve, arrange whole lettuce leaves on four salad plates. Place one artichoke heart in the center of each arrangement of lettuce leaves. Surround each artichoke heart with tomato slices alternating with egg slices and onion slices. Add some olives around each artichoke.

3. Prepare the vinaigrette by combining all the ingredients in a small bowl and mixing them well. Pour some over each salad.

ARTICHOKES GREEK STYLE

This dish can be served as an appetizer, as an accompaniment to the main course, or as a salad after the main course.

16 small artichokes
4 tablespoons lemon juice
8 tablespoons olive oil
1 bay leaf
a few sprigs fresh cilantro, finely chopped
salt and pepper to taste
2 ripe tomatoes, peeled, seeded, and sliced into
    small pieces

1. To prepare the artichokes for cooking, break off the leaves at the bottom and place an artichoke on a board sideways. Using a sharp knife, cut the lower leaves off up to where the heart of the artichoke is found. Then proceed to trim and cut off the leaves above the heart of the artichoke. Trim away the rest of the leaves, leaving the artichoke heart intact. When you finish trimming each artichoke, place the hearts in a casserole filled with cold water to cover and add the lemon juice. Leave the hearts in the lemon water for 30 minutes.

2. To cook the artichokes, remove them from the lemon water (reserving the water) and place them in a good-size frying pan with considerable depth. Add 6 tablespoons of the olive oil, the bay leaf, cilantro, and salt and pepper and cover up to the top of the artichokes with the lemon water. Cover the pan and cook the artichokes for about 15 minutes over medium-low heat, until they are tender. Allow them to cool in the frying pan with the remaining liquid.

3. Just before serving, drain the artichoke hearts with great care and place them in a good-size bowl. Add the tomatoes, a few extra drops of lemon juice, and 2 tablespoons of olive oil. Mix well and serve.

ARTICHOKE RAGOUT
(Ragoût d'artichauts)

This ragout makes an excellent appetizer any time of the year.

4–6 SERVINGS

10 fresh artichokes (or four 6-ounce cans artichokes in oil, well drained and rinsed in cold water)
4 tablespoons lemon juice
1 pound mushrooms
2 tablespoons butter
2 shallots, minced
4 sprigs fresh chervil, finely chopped
2 teaspoons flour or cornstarch
salt and pepper to taste

1. To prepare the artichokes for cooking, break off all the leaves at the bottom and place the artichoke on a board sideways. Using a sharp knife, cut the lower leaves off up to where the heart of the artichoke is found. Then proceed to trim away the leaves above the heart of the artichoke. Following the same procedure, cut off and trim the rest of the leaves, watching carefully that the artichoke heart remains intact. As each artichoke is trimmed, place the heart in a casserole filled with cold water and add the lemon juice. Leave the hearts in the lemon water for 30 minutes.

2. After 30 minutes, turn the heat to high under the casserole, and boil the artichokes for 12 minutes. (If you substitute canned artichokes, boil them only for 1 minute.) Drain them and set them aside. Remove the excess, hairy parts, and slice the remaining good parts evenly.

3. Clean and trim the mushrooms, cutting off only the stems and leaving the mushrooms whole.

4. Melt the butter in a deep skillet or frying pan. Add the artichoke hearts and mushrooms and sauté them lightly for 4–5 minutes.

5. After 5 minutes, add the chopped shallots and chervil, flour or cornstarch, salt and pepper, and mix all the ingredients thoroughly. Stir often. After 1–2 minutes, cover the skillet and turn off the heat. Serve the ragout warm.

ARTICHOKE SALAD

This dish can be served as a salad, an appetizer, or a main dish for lunch.

4 SERVINGS

12 fresh artichokes (or three 6-ounce cans artichokes in oil, well drained and rinsed in cold water)
4 hard-boiled eggs, sliced in quarters
4 tomatoes, sliced in quarters
12 black olives, pitted
1 small red onion, sliced in rings
fresh basil, finely chopped, as garnish

Vinaigrette
7 tablespoons olive oil
3 tablespoons balsamic vinegar
salt and freshly ground pepper to taste

1. If you are using fresh artichokes, prepare them as directed on page 19. If you are using canned artichokes, boil them for only 1 minute.

2. On four plates, evenly distribute the artichokes, eggs, tomatoes, and black olives. Scatter the onion rings on top.

3. Just before serving, prepare the vinaigrette by mixing all the ingredients well in a small bowl. Pour evenly over each dish, garnish with the basil, and serve.

ASPARAGUS

(Asparagus officinalis)

Asparagus was well known in antiquity; images of it have been found carved in the ancient Egyptian hieroglyphics. The Greeks used it as an aphrodisiac, and the Romans enriched a form of what we now call pasta by adding creamed asparagus to the flour, thus enhancing both the texture and the taste of the pasta.

However, for a long time after those early uses, asparagus was neglected in general cooking; it reappeared or was reintroduced in European kitchens around the eighteenth century. From Europe it traveled to America, where it has been widely cultivated and greatly appreciated at the table ever since. At the beginning of spring we feel exhilarated to see it arrive in large quantities at local markets and roadside produce stands.

There are several varieties of asparagus. In Europe, white asparagus is particularly cherished at the table. In North America that variety is less widely known, and the green asparagus is more typically served and savored. Asparagus stalks, like corn, taste best when they are eaten soon after they are picked; therefore, they should not be kept for a long time in the refrigerator. When choosing fresh asparagus in the market, select stalks that are firm with no trace of dryness or aging.

As with other vegetables, asparagus can be prepared in a variety of forms—creamed into a soup, for example, or served as whole stalks, hot or chilled or at room temperature. It is usually best served alone or separate from other dishes, so that its unique flavor can be appreciated. Thus, it is often served in the form of a soup or appetizer, as in some of the recipes presented here.

ASPARAGUS MILANESE

This is a perfect dish for a Sunday or festive brunch. It can also be served as a main dish, accompanied by plenty of fresh Italian bread, for a light supper in the springtime, when asparagus is in abundance.

4 SERVINGS

1 pound fresh asparagus
pinch salt
2 tablespoons lemon juice
$^1/_2$ cup grated Parmesan cheese
2 teaspoons butter
4 eggs
salt and freshly ground pepper to taste

1. Preheat the oven to 300°F. Gather the asparagus stalks into a bunch, all pointing the same way, and tie them with a string. Place them, tips up, in a good-size pot filled with boiling water, add the salt and lemon juice; blanch them for 4–5 minutes, until they become tender while remaining firm. Drain well.

2. Thoroughly butter a long, flat ovenproof dish and arrange the drained asparagus stalks carefully in it. Sprinkle the Parmesan cheese over the asparagus and place in the oven for about 10 minutes.

3. Just before serving, melt 2 teaspoons butter in a large skillet, break the eggs into it, and cook the whites well while retaining the freshness of the yolk. Sprinkle with salt and pepper.

4. Arrange the asparagus on warm plates, carefully placing one cooked egg on top of each serving. Serve immediately.

ASPARAGUS PUREE

This is an excellent accompaniment for egg, fish, and meat dishes.

4 SERVINGS

1 pound fresh asparagus
2 teaspoons lemon juice
2 shallots, minced
6 tablespoons dry white wine
1 (8-ounce container) crème fraîche or sour cream
salt and pepper to taste
3 teaspoons fresh tarragon, finely chopped

1. Trim the asparagus, peeling the hard parts and cutting off the ends. Place the asparagus in a large saucepan with salted water to cover and bring to a boil. Add the lemon juice and blanch the asparagus for 6–8 minutes until it becomes tender. Drain well.

2. Put the cooked asparagus in a food processor and puree thoroughly.

3. Place the shallots and white wine in a casserole and heat lightly on top of the stove; after a minute add the crème fraîche or sour cream. Stir continuously until the cream begins to bubble. At that point, add the pureed asparagus, salt and pepper, and tarragon; continue stirring until the ingredients are well mixed. Serve hot. If you want to make this in advance, butter an ovenproof dish and put the puree in it. Place in a warm oven to keep the puree hot until you are ready to serve it.

ASPARAGUS RISOTTO

This delicious risotto makes a wonderful main course when entertaining family or friends.

5 tablespoons butter or olive oil
1 medium onion, chopped
1 celery stalk, thinly sliced
1 cup fresh asparagus, cut into 1-inch pieces
2 cups Arborio rice
5 cups boiling water
1 bouillon cube (flavor of your choice)
1 cup dry white wine
salt and freshly ground black pepper to taste
$1/2$ teaspoon dried thyme
$1/2$ cup grated Parmesan or Romano cheese
additional grated cheese for the table

1. Melt the butter or heat the olive oil in a heavy, good-size saucepan. Add the onion, celery, and asparagus. Sauté lightly for about 3 minutes or until they begin to wilt. Add more butter or oil if necessary.

2. Add the rice and stir constantly for 1–2 minutes until it becomes well coated and changes color slightly. Add the boiling water gradually while stirring continuously. Add the bouillon cube and wine and continue stirring. Midway into the cooking, add the salt, pepper, and thyme and continue stirring until the rice is cooked, about 15 minutes.

3. When the rice is cooked, add the grated cheese and stir vigorously until it is all incorporated into the rice. Serve the risotto hot and place additional grated cheese on the table.

ASPARAGUS BATONNETS

Serve the batonnets as an appetizer or as an accompaniment to the main course.

20 stalks fresh asparagus (5 per person), trimmed
8 tablespoons flour
2 eggs, beaten
3/4 cup bread crumbs
vegetable oil (as needed for frying)

1. Preheat the oven to 200°F. Cut the asparagus into pieces 6–7 inches long, discarding the tough bottom ends. Place the asparagus pieces in salted boiling water to cover and cook for 5–6 minutes. Drain the asparagus, rinse in cold water, and dry with paper towels.

2. With great care, roll each asparagus piece first in the flour, then in the eggs, and then in the bread crumbs.

3. Fill a skillet with approximately half an inch of oil. Turn the heat to medium-high until the oil is hot. Place the asparagus pieces, four at a time, in the oil and cook carefully, watching that they are fried on all sides and at the same time remain intact.

4. When each batch of asparagus is done, place in a well-buttered ovenproof dish and keep hot in the preheated oven for 10–15 minutes until you are ready to serve.

ASPARAGUS SALAD MIMOSA

4 SERVINGS

20 fresh asparagus stalks, trimmed
1 small head Boston lettuce
2 cups cooked beets, sliced julienne style
4 hard-boiled eggs, chopped

Vinaigrette
8 tablespoons olive oil
4 tablespoons cider vinegar
1 teaspoon French mustard (Dijon or other)
1 shallot, minced
salt and pepper to taste

1. Bring salted water to a boil in a large saucepan. Add the trimmed asparagus and cook for about 3 minutes. Drain and rinse the asparagus under cold water. Drain again and set it aside.

2. Rinse and dry the lettuce leaves well. Set them aside.

3. On each of four salad plates, arrange three leaves of lettuce. Place five asparagus stalks on top and place the beets on both sides of the asparagus. Distribute the chopped hard-boiled eggs evenly over each serving.

4. Prepare the vinaigrette by mixing together all the ingredients in a small bowl. Just before serving, pour some of the vinaigrette over each salad and serve immediately.

Saint Michael Asparagus Soup

$1/2$ pound fresh asparagus, tough ends removed, cut into
　　1-inch lengths
1 potato, peeled and diced
4 shallots, sliced
2 medium carrots, sliced
1 cup half-and-half
2 tablespoons butter or margarine
salt and pepper to taste

1. Bring water to a boil in a large saucepan. Add the vegetables and cook until tender. Put the mixture in a blender and whirl it until smooth.

2. Return the mixture to the pot, add the half-and-half, butter, and salt and pepper. Bring to a simmer while stirring. Cover the pot and let it simmer for 10 minutes. Serve hot.

AVOCADOS

(Persea americana)

The avocado, contrary to popular belief, is not a vegetable but a fruit. The confusion stems from the frequent culinary use of the avocado as a vegetable. It is primarily served in salty dishes and seldom in a sweet fashion as a dessert, at least not in the United States. Suffice to say that in this collection I resort to common local use and treat it exclusively as a vegetable.

The avocado tree has been cultivated for centuries in the Caribbean Islands and in Central and South America. In the twentieth century, its cultivation extended to other areas of the world such as Israel, Turkey, South Africa, Australia, and here in the United States where the climate warrants its growth, such as in Florida and California. As market demand for the avocado increases, its cultivation for commercial use continues to extend to other parts of the world.

The original Aztec name for the avocado is ahuacatt; that was transformed into the Spanish aguacate and the English avocado. The avocado fruit is oval or round, depending on its variety. Its inside flesh is usually yellow or pale green, developed around a large simple seed. Among the many varieties of avocado fruit, there are three that are more well known than the others. They differ according to their place of origin: Mexico, Central America (mostly Guatemala), and the Caribbean Islands.

The avocado fruit contains a high degree of fat (sometimes as much as 25 percent). It is rich in vitamin A, protein, riboflavin, and thiamine and has gained great popularity among vegetarians, who benefit immensely from using the avocado to balance their diet.

Because avocados in general don't have a long life expectancy and tend to ripen and discolor quickly, it is important that they be served as soon as possible after they are peeled and sliced. One way to preserve them and prolong their appearance is to mix them well with lemon juice. The lemon juice not only acts as a preservative but also enhances the avocado's nutty flavor and makes it more distinct.

Avocado and Tofu Dip

This healthy and nutritious dip can be served with Mexican corn tortillas, melba toast, or ordinary crackers.

3 SERVINGS

2 ripe avocados, peeled
1/2 pound tofu
1 tablespoon paprika
2 tablespoons lemon juice
2 tablespoons olive oil
2 shallots or 1 small onion, minced
4 tablespoons fresh cilantro, minced
salt and pepper to taste

Mix all the ingredients in a food processor and whirl for a few seconds. Adjust the seasonings as desired and place the mixture in a bowl. Refrigerate until you are ready to serve.

Avocado and Mâche Salad

This salad is best as an appetizer for lunch or brunch. It is particularly attractive when you harvest the fresh mâche and peas from your garden. If mâche is unavailable, one may substitute baby spinach leaves for this recipe.

4 SERVINGS

4 small avocados, peeled and sliced lengthwise
1 large bunch mâche leaves, washed and dried
1 cup fresh or frozen peas (large)
1 shallot, minced
4 small cucumbers, sliced

Vinaigrette
5 tablespoons walnut or sesame oil
3 tablespoons lemon juice
pinch paprika
salt and freshly ground pepper to taste

1. Place the vegetables in a large salad bowl.

2. Prepare the vinaigrette by mixing all the ingredients well in a small bowl. When you are ready to serve the salad, pour the vinaigrette over the vegetables in the bowl and gently toss a few times until they are well coated. Serve immediately.

Saints Peter and Paul Avocado Soup

This soup is often served in our monastery during the summer months, especially on June 29, the feast of the great apostles Peter and Paul, foundation stones of the Church of God, whose icons are venerated in our chapel.

4–6 SERVINGS

3 leeks, white parts only, trimmed and sliced
3 avocados, peeled and sliced in half
3 tablespoons lemon juice
1 (8-ounce) container low-fat sour cream
1 teaspoon paprika
salt and pepper to taste
lemon rind as garnish

1. Place the leeks in a saucepan, cover with 6 cups water, and bring to a boil. Lower the heat to medium-low and cook the leeks for 15–20 minutes. Remove pan from the heat, allow to cool slightly, and then whirl leeks and water in a blender or food processor. Pour the mixture back into the pan or into a large bowl.

2. Place the avocados, lemon juice, sour cream, paprika, and salt and pepper in the blender or food processor and whirl for about 1 minute. Add to the leek mixture and blend all the ingredients well by hand. Place in the refrigerator for at least 2 hours before serving. Serve cold and add some lemon rind on the top of each serving as garnish.

Avocado Salad with Goat Cheese

This is a delightful and nutritious appetizer year round.

4 SERVINGS

1 small head Bibb lettuce, washed and drained
1 (8-ounce) log of goat cheese, cut into 4 slices
2 avocados, peeled and sliced in half lengthwise
fresh cilantro and chives, finely chopped, as garnish

Vinaigrette
6 tablespoons olive oil
3 tablespoons lemon juice
salt and pepper to taste

1. Preheat the oven to 350°F. Separate the lettuce leaves and arrange on four individual salad plates.

2. Place the goat cheese in the oven on a cookie sheet for 5 minutes, or until it begins to melt.

3. While the cheese is in the oven, place an avocado half on top of the lettuce on each plate.

4. Prepare the vinaigrette by mixing all the ingredients well in a small bowl. When the cheese is ready, place a slice on each avocado half. Pour some of the vinaigrette over each serving and sprinkle cilantro and chives on top as garnish.

Guacamole

4 SERVINGS

4 ripe avocados, peeled and mashed
2 tomatoes, peeled, seeded, and chopped
1 medium onion, diced
1 small red pepper, diced
1 small green pepper, diced
3 tablespoons fresh cilantro, finely chopped
2 tablespoons sour cream (or plain yogurt)
2 tablespoons lemon juice
salt and freshly ground pepper to taste

1. Place the avocado in a deep bowl. Add the tomatoes, onion, peppers, and cilantro. Mix the ingredients well.

2. Add the sour cream, lemon juice, and salt and pepper to taste. Mix all the ingredients again very well. Cover the bowl tightly with plastic wrap and place in the refrigerator until serving time.

BEANS

(Phaseolus vulgaris)

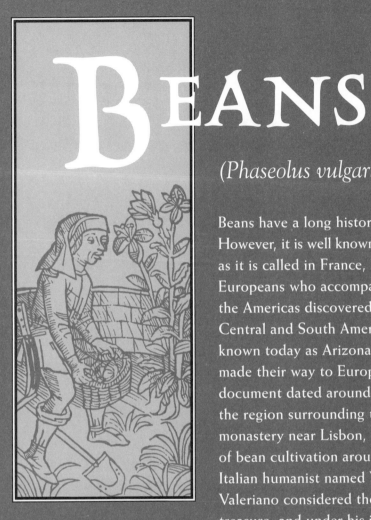

Beans have a long history, dating back to the ancient Greeks and Romans. However, it is well known that the popular common garden bean, or haricot, as it is called in France, had its origin on the American continent. The Europeans who accompanied Christopher Columbus upon his arrival in the Americas discovered the bean, first in Cuba and later in other parts of Central and South America, as well as areas of North America, in what is known today as Arizona and Utah. From these American sources, beans made their way to Europe. In France, the first mention of beans is in a document dated around 1564, which relates that beans were cultivated in the region surrounding the town of Vienne, having been introduced from a monastery near Lisbon, Portugal. In Italy, we find mention of the first traces of bean cultivation around 1528 in the town of Belluno, where a certain Italian humanist named Valeriano started sowing beans imported from Peru. Valeriano considered the discovery of beans similar to the discovery of a treasure, and under his influence bean agriculture was extended to other regions of Italy. By the end of the sixteenth century, the cultivation and lore of beans were well established throughout Italy, France, and Spain. These regions were the basis for the further expansion of beans to other areas of the world.

Today, a great many varieties of beans are cultivated by serious gardeners all around the globe. Beans have become an integral part of the daily diet because they are rich in vitamin C, potassium, and calcium and are an excellent source of protein; they provide an essential substitute for meat in many vegetarian diets. Beans are sometimes divided into two categories: fresh or green beans harvested from the garden and eaten in their entirety (the pod along with the beans); and dried beans, which are harvested at the end of the season, then snapped from their shells, left out to dry, and preserved for future use in dry sealed containers. The following recipes incorporate various types of beans in both of these two forms. Among the twenty-nine principal types, green and yellow wax beans, haricots verts, lima beans, and romano pole beans are cultivated yearly in our garden. Among the dried beans used frequently at the monastic table and therefore represented in this collection of recipes are fava beans, white navy beans, black beans, and lentils. Note that for these recipes one can of beans is equal to one cup of freshly shelled beans.

GREEN BEAN SALAD

This dish can be served as an appetizer or as a salad after a main course.

1^1/2 pounds French green beans (or regular string beans)
^{1}/2 pound fresh mushrooms, sliced thin
2 shallots, minced
1 lemon
1 (8-ounce) container low-fat yogurt
salt and freshly ground pepper to taste

1. Trim the green beans and place them in a saucepan with cold water to cover for 10 minutes.

2. Place the pan on the stove and bring the water to a boil. Then lower the heat to medium-low and cook the beans for 10 minutes. Drain and rinse in cold water. Set aside.

3. Squeeze the juice of the lemon into a bowl, add the yogurt and salt and pepper and whisk thoroughly by hand or with a mixer until the mixture turns into a smooth dressing.

4. When you are ready to serve, add the beans, mushrooms, and shallots to the bowl of dressing. Mix well and serve.

WAX BEAN PUREE

This puree makes a wonderful accompaniment to fish and meat dishes.

6 SERVINGS

2 pounds wax beans (preferably new tender beans), trimmed and broken in half
1 shallot, minced
1 (8-ounce) container Crème Fraîche or light cream
6 tablespoons butter
salt and pepper to taste
parsley, finely chopped, as garnish

1. Cook the beans in a large saucepan in salted boiling water for 10–12 minutes. Drain beans and rinse in cold water. Puree beans in a food processor until they turn into a smooth cream. Add the shallot and process the cream a bit more.

2. Heat the crème fraîche in a saucepan and allow it to reduce a bit over low heat.

3. Melt the butter in a deep frying pan. After 1–2 minutes, add the bean puree. Stir and slowly add the reduced crème fraîche and salt and pepper. Mix well and cover the frying pan for 1–2 minutes. Sprinkle some parsley on top of each serving as garnish. Serve hot.

Green Beans Portuguese Style

This recipe can also be used with wax beans if you prefer them to green beans.

4–6 SERVINGS

1 pound green beans
pinch salt
4 tablespoons olive oil or lard
4 large tomatoes, peeled and cubed
salt and pepper to taste
parsley, chopped, as garnish

1. Trim the beans and place them in a saucepan with cold water to cover for 15 minutes. Then place the pan on the stove and bring the water to a boil. Add salt, lower the heat to medium-low, cover the pan, and cook the beans for about 10 minutes. They should remain firm and not be overcooked. Drain and rinse in cold water. Set aside.

2. Pour the olive oil into a large, deep skillet, add the cubed tomatoes and salt and pepper. Sauté the tomatoes briefly until they turn into a light sauce. Be careful not to overcook them. Add the green beans and mix well with the tomato sauce until the beans are hot again (1–2 minutes). Serve hot with the parsley as garnish.

Spicy Black Beans

6–8 SERVINGS

1 pound black beans (dried or canned)
$^1/_3$ cup vegetable oil
3 onions, sliced
8 large tomatoes, peeled and chopped
4 garlic cloves, minced
2 celery stalks, finely sliced
1 jalapeño pepper, seeded and sliced
2 green bell peppers, seeded and sliced
$^1/_3$ cup chopped fresh cilantro
$^1/_3$ cup finely chopped fresh parsley
1 teaspoon cumin
1 teaspoon chili powder
salt and pepper to taste

1. Soak dried beans overnight. Rinse in cold water. Cook beans in salted boiling water for 45 minutes. Discard the water. Put fresh water in the saucepan and boil again for about 20 minutes. Drain beans and discard the water. This process can be avoided by using an amount of canned beans equal to the amount of dried. If you use canned beans, they need to be rinsed in cold water and drained. Set beans aside.

2. Heat the oil in a saucepan and add the onions, tomatoes, garlic, celery, peppers, cilantro, and parsley. Sauté the vegetables over medium heat for 4–5 minutes, until they gradually turn into a sauce. Lower the heat to medium-low and add the spices and salt and pepper. Stir well and cover the saucepan. Cook for another 12–15 minutes, stirring from time to time.

3. Preheat the oven to 350°F. Add the beans to the vegetables and mix everything well. Butter or oil an ovenproof dish thoroughly and place the bean mixture in it. Cover the dish and place it in the oven for 30 minutes. Serve hot.

Fava Bean Ragout

This dish can be served alone or on top of white rice, which makes a delicious combination and provides protein, as well.

2 (15-ounce) cans fava beans (or the equivalent in fresh beans from the garden or market)
6 tablespoons olive oil
5 garlic cloves, peeled and crushed but remaining whole
1 large onion, minced
1 branch fresh rosemary
6 medium ripe tomatoes, peeled and sliced
salt and freshly ground pepper to taste

1. Drain and rinse the canned beans in cold water. Rinse again and set aside.

2. Add the olive oil to a large cast-iron pot and turn heat to medium-low; add the garlic and onion and sauté for about 2 minutes. Add the rosemary, tomatoes, and salt and pepper and cook over low heat for 8–10 minutes. Stir frequently.

3. After 10 minutes, add the fava beans, stir all the ingredients well, and continue cooking for 5 more minutes. Check the seasonings, remove the rosemary branch, and serve hot.

FAVA BEANS WITH SMALL ONIONS

6–8 SERVINGS

$^1/_2$ pound fava beans in pods
$^1/_2$ pound pearl onions (fresh or frozen)
10 tablespoons olive oil
6 tablespoons lemon juice
$2^1/_2$ cups water
salt and pepper to taste
fresh parsley, finely chopped, as desired

1. Remove the beans from their pods. Peel the onions if you are using fresh ones. If necessary, you may use canned onions.

2. Pour the olive oil into a cast-iron saucepan. Heat the oil over medium-low heat and then add the beans and onions. Sauté for 1 minute, stirring continuously. Add the lemon juice, water (more if needed), and salt and pepper. Stir a few times and then cover the pan. Reduce the heat to low and simmer gently for 1–$1^1/_4$ hours. Stir occasionally. The dish is done when the water has all but evaporated. Check the seasonings and add an extra touch of olive oil and the fresh parsley. Mix well and serve.

Fava Beans Greek Style

This is an excellent dish to serve during the harvest or cold weather months

4–6 SERVINGS

1/2 pound fava beans, fresh or dried
5 tablespoons Greek olive oil or other similar
2 pounds fresh garden spinach or Swiss chard, trimmed
    and cleaned well
4 large garlic cloves, minced
1/2 cup Greek black olives, sliced
2 teaspoons dried thyme
salt and pepper to taste
1/2 cup crumbled feta cheese

1. Preheat the oven to 350°F.

2. Cook the fava beans according to directions. If they are fresh from the garden, cook them for 12–15 minutes in salty water until tender. Drain thoroughly in a colander and set aside. Reserve the cooking liquid.

3. Thoroughly oil a baking dish and pour into it 1 cup of the reserved cooking liquid.

4. Pour 2 tablespoons olive oil in a large skillet over medium-high heat. Add 1/3 cup of the cooking liquid, and cook the spinach or Swiss chard for 4–5 minutes or until wilted. Stir continuously. Remove the greens from the heat and allow them to cool a bit; then chop coarsely.

4. Pour the remaining 3 tablespoons of olive oil into the skillet, add the minced garlic, and cook for half a minute or so while stirring continuously. Add the cooked greens, olives, and thyme and stir to combine well. Remove from heat and add salt and pepper to taste.

5. In the greased baking dish spread a layer of the fava beans. On the top of the fava beans spread the greens mixture. Spread feta cheese over the top and drizzle with olive oil. Bake for about 30 minutes. Remove from the oven and serve hot.

ROMANO POLE BEANS AND ORECCHIETTE

6 SERVINGS

60 fresh pole beans (the flat Romano type)
1 pound orecchiette pasta
7 tablespoons olive oil
5 garlic cloves, peeled
15 fresh basil leaves
1/2 cup heavy cream
salt and freshly ground pepper to taste
grated Romano cheese for the table

1. Trim beans and cook in boiling salted water for about 5 minutes. Rinse in cold water and set aside.

2. Cook the pasta in abundant boiling water (add some salt and 1 tablespoon of olive oil) for 5–6 minutes, making sure that it remains al dente. When the pasta is done, drain thoroughly.

3. While the pasta is cooking, prepare the sauce by placing the remaining 6 tablespoons of olive oil, garlic, and basil in a food processor and blending thoroughly. Pour this mixture into a large saucepan, add the cream and salt and pepper, and cook for 1 to 2 minutes over medium-low heat. When the sauce is very hot, add the pasta and the beans and mix gently.

4. Serve immediately and present plenty of grated cheese at the table.

POLE BEAN SALAD

This is an inviting appetizer for lunch or supper, especially during the summer and early fall months. French-style string beans (haricots verts) can be substituted for the pole beans if necessary.

6 SERVINGS

60 pole beans (the flat Romano type)
6 medium tomatoes, sliced
1 small red onion, thinly sliced
fresh basil, chopped, as garnish

Vinaigrette
6 tablespoons olive oil
3 tablespoons balsamic vinegar
salt and pepper to taste

1. Trim the beans but leave them intact otherwise. Boil in salted water for 5 minutes. Rinse in cold water and then drain. Set aside.

2. Mix together the ingredients for the vinaigrette.

3. Distribute the beans onto six serving plates (about 10 beans per person), on one side of the plate. Put the tomato slices on the other side and some sliced onion in the center. Just before serving, pour the vinaigrette over the vegetables (add more oil and vinegar if needed). Sprinkle the basil on top of each serving as garnish and serve.

WHITE BEANS SPANISH STYLE

This dish may be served as a main course accompanied by plain rice. The combination of rice and beans provides a complete protein and is a meal in itself.

5 tablespoons olive oil
1 large onion, sliced
1 red pepper, diced
1 yellow pepper, diced
3 garlic cloves, minced
2 cups tomato sauce, homemade or otherwise
1 tablespoon Worcestershire sauce
$^1/_2$ cup dry sherry
1 bay leaf
salt and pepper to taste
2 cups cooked white beans or well-drained and rinsed
   canned beans
grated Parmesan cheese for topping

1. Pour the olive oil into a large skillet, add the onion and peppers, and sauté over medium-low heat for 4–5 minutes. Add the garlic, tomato sauce, Worcestershire sauce, sherry, bay leaf, and salt and pepper and continue cooking for 15–20 minutes. Stir frequently.

2. Preheat the oven to 300°F. Add the beans to the other ingredients and mix well.

3. Remove the bay leaf and place the bean mixture in a long, flat, well-buttered baking dish. Top with Parmesan cheese and bake for about 30 minutes. Serve hot.

Lima Bean Soup Tuscan Style

7 cups water
1 pound green lima beans, fresh or frozen
6 tablespoons olive oil
1 medium Vidalia onion, coarsely chopped
1 large carrot, diced
1 celery stalk, diced
6 garlic cloves, minced
pinch salt
6 medium tomatoes, peeled and diced
sea salt and freshly ground pepper to taste
$1/3$ cup chopped fresh basil
freshly grated Parmesan for serving

1. Soak the beans in a large soup pot in simmering water over medium-low heat for 12–15 minutes. When tender but firm, remove beans from heat; drain and set aside.

2. Heat the olive oil over medium heat in a medium saucepan or nonstick skillet and add the onion, carrot, and celery. Cook, stirring, until tender, 7–8 minutes. Add the garlic and salt and continue to cook, stirring, until the garlic begins to turn golden, 1–2 minutes. Add the tomatoes and turn up the heat slightly. Cook, stirring often, until they have cooked down to a lovely sauce, 12–15 minutes.

3. Season the sauce to taste with salt and pepper and stir it into the beans. Turn the heat to medium-low, cover the pot, and simmer for 30 minutes, stirring from time to time. If need be, adjust seasonings. Stir in the basil. Drizzle some extra olive oil over the top and serve hot. Garnish as desired with grated cheese.

SAINT BERNARD CHICKPEA SALAD

This salad can be served at room temperature during the cold weather months or chilled in the refrigerator for an hour and served cold during the hot weather months.

4 SERVINGS

1 (15-ounce) can chickpeas, drained and rinsed
1 long cucumber, peeled and cut in small even dice
2 celery stalks, thinly sliced
1 medium red onion, finely chopped
1 garlic clove, minced
8 fresh basil leaves, chopped (if basil is not available, use parsley)
2 tablespoons grated Parmesan cheese
2 tablespoons olive oil
2 tablespoons white or rosé wine vinegar
salt and freshly ground pepper to taste

1. In a large salad bowl, place the chickpeas, cucumber, celery, onion, garlic, and basil. Toss the ingredients gently and set aside.

2. Just before serving, add the Parmesan cheese, pour the oil and vinegar over the salad, add salt and pepper to taste, and toss all ingredients once more until they are evenly coated with the oil and vinegar.

LENTILS BURGUNDY STYLE

This is an excellent dish to serve with plain white rice or to accompany a meat or egg dish.

6–8 SERVINGS

1 pound dried lentils (French, if possible)
2 thin carrots, finely sliced
1 large onion, minced
3 garlic cloves, minced
1 bouquet garni (thyme, laurel, and parsley)
3 cups red wine (preferably from Burgundy)
2 cups water, plus more if needed
salt and pepper to taste

1. Soak the lentils in cold water for 5–6 hours and then drain.

2. Place the lentils, carrots, onion, garlic, and bouquet garni in a large cast-iron saucepan. Add the wine, water, and salt and pepper and bring to a boil.

3. When the mixture begins to boil, stir thoroughly, reduce the heat to medium-low, cover the pan, and cook slowly for 1–1 1/2 hours. Stir from time to time, check the seasonings, and add more water if needed. Make sure the mixture does not burn at the bottom.

4. When the lentils are well cooked and the liquid has evaporated, remove the bouquet garni and serve immediately.

Saint Maur Black-Eyed Pea Salad

4 SERVINGS

1 (15-ounce) can black-eyed peas, drained and rinsed
1 small Vidalia onion (or similar), sliced in half moons
1 cup fresh baby spinach (or arugula), washed and dried
1 bell pepper, sliced in thin strips
1 large garlic clove, minced
1/3 cup finely chopped fresh cilantro
2 tablespoons olive oil
2 tablespoons cider vinegar or lemon juice
sea salt and freshly ground pepper to taste

1. Place the black-eyed peas in a large salad bowl. Add the onion, spinach, pepper strips, garlic, and cilantro. Toss thoroughly.

2. Just before serving, pour the olive oil and vinegar or lemon juice over the salad and add salt and pepper to taste. Toss the salad gently and serve at room temperature.

Saint Francis Lentils Gratin

4–6 SERVINGS

4 tablespoons olive oil
1 onion, diced
1 carrot, sliced
1 celery stalk, sliced
2 cups lentils
4 garlic cloves, minced
salt and pepper to taste
5 cups water
2 eggs
$^1/_3$ cup milk
$^1/_3$ cup bread crumbs
$^1/_2$ cup grated cheese (Parmesan or similar)
2 tablespoons chopped fresh parsley
1 tablespoon dried thyme (or 3 tablespoons fresh,
    if available)

1. Pour the oil into a large saucepan and add the onion, carrot, and celery. Sauté over medium-low heat for about 2 minutes. Add the lentils, garlic, salt and pepper, and water and boil for 30 minutes over medium heat. Stir from time to time. When the lentils are tender, if any water remains, drain them in a colander.

2. Preheat the oven to 300°F. Beat the eggs in a large bowl. Add the milk and beat some more. Add the bread crumbs, $^1/_4$ cup cheese, and herbs and mix well. Add the cooked lentils and vegetables and mix thoroughly.

3. Butter a flat baking dish and pour the mixture into it. Using a spatula, smooth out the surface of the mixture. Sprinkle the remaining $^1/_4$ cup cheese on top. Bake for about 30 minutes. Serve hot during the cold months or refrigerate and serve cold during warm weather.

CREAMY LENTIL SOUP

4–6 SERVINGS

4 tablespoons olive oil
2 onions, chopped
2 carrots, sliced
1 1/2 cups lentils
8 cups water
1 bay leaf
1 sprig thyme
chopped parsley, as desired
salt and pepper to taste
1 egg yolk
1/2 cup milk
olive oil
4 garlic cloves, minced
garlicky croutons, as garnish

1. Pour the olive oil into a soup pot and sauté the onions and carrots over medium-low heat for 2 minutes.

2. Add the lentils, water, bay leaf, thyme, parsley, and salt and pepper. Bring the water to a boil, cover the pot, and let simmer over low heat for 1 1/4 hours. In the meantime, place the egg yolk in a deep bowl, add the milk, and beat well, using a mixer if you like. Put this mixture aside.

3. Let the soup cool. Remove the bay leaf and thyme. Then pass the soup through a sieve or blend in a food processor. Return the soup to a clean pot and reheat. When the soup is hot, add the egg mixture. Stir and blend well. Cover the pot.

4. Pour some olive oil into a small frying pan and sauté the minced garlic for a quick second, stirring continuously. Let the garlic get golden, but do not let it burn. Add the garlic to the soup. Stir and blend thoroughly. Serve hot, adding croutons on top of each serving as garnish.

BEETS

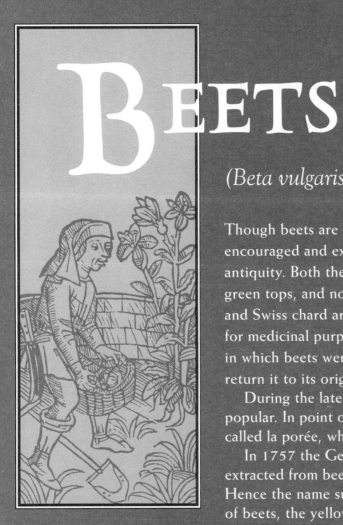

(Beta vulgaris)

Though beets are African in origin, it was the Greeks and Romans who encouraged and expanded their cultivation during the period of late antiquity. Both the Greeks and the Romans cultivated beets mostly for the green tops, and not the roots. The greens were used very much as spinach and Swiss chard are used today; besides their culinary use, they were used for medicinal purposes, such as a remedy for constipation. Also, the water in which beets were boiled was sometimes added to wine gone sour, to return it to its original taste.

During the late Middle Ages the beet root became more and more popular. In point of fact, it became, in France, the main ingredient of a soup called la porée, which was the most popular of all the soups of that period.

In 1757 the German chemist Andreas Marggraf identified the sugar extracted from beets as similar to the sugar extracted from sugar cane. Hence the name sugar beet. For this reason, appreciation for both types of beets, the yellow and the red, increased, and beet cultivation was expanded throughout Europe. In France alone, during the time of the Emperor Napoleon, 42,000 hectares of beet plantation were exclusively cultivated for the production of sugar for the country. Even today, when roaming around the French countryside during harvest time, one is impressed to see tall piles of beets on the roadside waiting to be transported to large production plants where eventually they will be converted into pure sugar.

RED BEET SALAD WITH ROQUEFORT CHEESE

This is an elegant appetizer any time of the year and especially delicious during the hot weather months.

6 medium beets
2 apples
1 bunch mâche (or baby spinach or baby arugula)
1 Belgian endive, sliced in 1-inch strips
chives, finely chopped, as garnish

Dressing
4 ounces sour cream
$^1/_2$ cup crumbled Roquefort cheese
1 small red onion, minced
4 tablespoons lemon juice
2 tablespoons olive oil
pinch toasted sesame seeds (optional)
salt and freshly ground pepper to taste

1. Boil the beets for 8–10 minutes. Rinse them in cold water. Peel the beets and slice them julienne style. Peel the apples and also slice them julienne style. Place beets and apples in a salad bowl and refrigerate until you are ready to serve.

2. Wash and dry the mâche leaves. Place them in a separate bowl. Add the sliced endive.

3. Mix all the dressing ingredients well in a small bowl. Beat by hand until the dressing acquires a creamy consistency. Refrigerate until needed.

4. When you are ready to serve, set out the serving plates. Divide the dressing between the two bowls of vegetables and gently toss the salads until the vegetables are well coated. Serve the beets and apples on one half of the plate and the mâche and endive on the other half. Sprinkle the chives over everything as garnish.

BABY BEET SALAD

If the potatoes or beets are a bit too big to serve whole, they can be sliced in perfect halves and served. When possible, however, they should be presented whole. This is an excellent appetizer any time of the year, but especially in midsummer, when the baby beets and small potatoes are fresh and tender.

4 SERVINGS

12 small beets
12 small potatoes, peeled
16 small onions (cippolina, shallots, or similar), peeled
fresh chives, finely chopped, as garnish

Vinaigrette
8 tablespoons olive oil
3 tablespoons white vinegar
salt and freshly ground pepper to taste
2 teaspoons French mustard (Dijon or other)

1. Trim the beets at both ends. Boil them in salted water for 25–30 minutes, or until they are tender when pierced with a fork. Drain and rinse under cold water. Peel the beets and set aside.

2. In salted water, boil the peeled potatoes and onions separately for about 20 minutes. The potatoes should be cooked but not overcooked; they should remain firm and whole. The same applies to the onions. Drain the vegetables and allow them to cool.

3. When you are ready to serve, place the beets, potatoes, and onions in a deep salad bowl. Prepare the vinaigrette by mixing all the ingredients well in a small bowl. Pour this over the vegetables and toss gently. Garnish the top with the chives and serve.

BEETS DIJON STYLE

Beets thus prepared are a good accompaniment to fish and egg main courses.

4–6 SERVINGS

1 pound beets, peeled and diced
2 tablespoons white vermouth
$^{1}/_{2}$ cup heavy cream
2 tablespoons Dijon mustard
salt and pepper to taste
fresh chervil, finely chopped, as garnish

1. Boil the diced beets in salted water for 7–8 minutes. Drain and set aside.

2. When you are ready to serve, prepare a sauce by combining in a saucepan the vermouth, cream, mustard, and salt and pepper. Mix well and heat over low heat. Add the beets and stir continuously for about 1 minute until they are reheated. Serve immediately garnished with the chervil.

COLD BEET SOUP

This soup makes an ideal appetizer for a hot summer day.

6–8 SERVINGS

2 quarts water
6 large fresh beets, peeled and diced
2 leeks, white parts only, sliced
2 shallots, chopped
2 celery stalks, finely sliced
1 bouillon cube (flavor of your choice)
2 teaspoons granulated sugar
salt and pepper to taste
2 (8-ounce) containers plain low-fat yogurt
1 medium cucumber, peeled, seeded, and finely chopped
fresh dill, finely chopped, to taste
1 bunch fresh chives, finely chopped

1. Bring 2 quarts water to a boil in a soup pot and add the vegetables, bouillon cube, and sugar. Cover the pot and cook slowly for 30 minutes over medium-low heat.

2. After 30 minutes, add salt and pepper, stir well, and remove the pot from the heat. Let stand for 30 minutes to cool. Blend the soup in a blender or food processor and then place it in a container in the refrigerator for several hours or even a day before serving.

3. Place the yogurt in a deep bowl, add the cucumber, dill, and chives and mix well by hand. Cover and place in the refrigerator until you are ready to serve. Just before serving, blend the creamy beet soup and the yogurt mixture. Serve cold.

BEETS RÉMOULADE

These beets go well with hard-boiled eggs and tomato slices on the side.

4 SERVINGS

6 medium red beets, peeled and sliced julienne style
1 small onion, sliced julienne style
5 tablespoons lemon juice
1 egg yolk
2 tablespoons French mustard (Dijon or other)
$1/2$ cup olive oil
1 tablespoon tarragon-scented vinegar
salt and pepper to taste

1. Cook the sliced beets and onion for 1 minute in salted boiling water and drain completely. Place the vegetables in a deep bowl and add the lemon juice. Mix well and refrigerate for at least 2 hours before serving.

2. Place the egg yolk in another deep bowl and add the mustard. Then gradually add the oil as you whisk the mixture by hand or with a mixer. Add the vinegar and salt and pepper and mix until the sauce achieves an even consistency. Keep refrigerated until needed.

3. When you are ready to serve, blend the beets and onion with the sauce. Serve cold as an appetizer.

Cabbage, Broccoli, Brussels Sprouts & Cauliflower

(Brassica oleracea)

All these vegetables are members of the same Brassica extraction. The cabbage is considered one of the oldest and better-known vegetables of early antiquity. Some claim its place of origin, at least in its wild state, to be the European coast of the Atlantic Ocean and the Mediterranean Sea. Others claim the cabbage originated on the Asiatic continent. Whatever its exact origins may be, the cabbage and its derivatives were highly esteemed by the people of ancient times. The Germans and the Celts especially were avid cultivators of all types of cabbage, and the Romans were not far behind. The Romans used it as a means to overcome a melancholic state and as an antidote against alcohol, especially before attending the lavish banquets and wild parties for which they were famous, and at which inordinate amounts of alcohol were consumed. This tradition survives to this day. In certain countries of Eastern Europe, cabbage leaves are eaten as a remedy after heavy consumption of vodka. In France, there is a special cabbage soup that is used as a remedy after heavy wine drinking.

The vegetables of the cabbage family are particularly important because they are rich in vitamins, minerals, calcium, magnesium, and sulfites. In our time, there are many theories in the health community that seriously encourage the inclusion of these vegetables in our daily diet as a way to fight cancer. Recent studies have shown that a diet rich in cruciferous vegetables such as broccoli and cauliflower definitely lowers the risk of cancer, especially when consumed in significant amounts on a weekly basis.

Two-Cabbage Salad

This salad can be served as an appetizer, or it can be served after the main course.

6–8 SERVINGS

$^1/_2$ medium white cabbage, minced
$^1/_2$ medium red cabbage, minced
4 clementines, peeled and separated into segments
$^1/_2$ cup sliced almonds, roasted (roast in the oven at 300°F for 15 minutes)
$^1/_2$ cup small chunks blue cheese (Blue d'Auvergne if possible)

Salad Dressing
$^1/_3$ cup olive oil
4 tablespoons fresh lemon juice
salt and freshly ground pepper to taste

1. Place the cabbage in a deep salad bowl. Add the clementines, almonds, and blue cheese.

2. Prepare the salad dressing by mixing all the ingredients well in a small bowl. Just before serving, pour the dressing over the salad. Toss the salad and serve it at room temperature.

Creamy Cabbage

This dish accompanies egg and meat dishes well. On a special occasion, it can be served as an appetizer.

6 SERVINGS

1 large white cabbage, trimmed
1 (4-ounce) stick butter
3 carrots, sliced
1 large Bermuda onion, sliced
salt and pepper to taste
5 tablespoons flour or cornstarch
2 cups milk

1. Slice the cabbage into 6 even chunks, making sure that each one remains intact. Place them carefully in a saucepan with boiling water to cover. Boil for 2–3 minutes. Drain carefully so they remain whole. Rinse in cold water.

2. Melt half of the butter in a good-size pot. Add the carrots and onion and cook over low heat for 4–5 minutes. Then carefully add the cabbage chunks and 2 cups of water. Sprinkle on some salt, stir, cover the pot, and cook slowly over low heat for 25–30 minutes.

3. In the meantime, preheat the oven to 350°F. Prepare a béchamel sauce in a separate saucepan by first melting the rest of the butter and then adding the flour or cornstarch and stirring continuously until they are well mixed. Add the milk and salt and pepper, and stir continuously over low heat for 2 minutes until the sauce is the right consistency.

4. When the cabbage and other vegetables are cooked, place them with great care in a well-buttered, long, flat, ovenproof baking dish. Pour the béchamel sauce over all the vegetables. Place the dish in the oven for 15 minutes. Serve hot.

Monastery-Style Cabbage Coleslaw

This basic coleslaw, besides being nutritious, is an excellent dish to serve during the hot days of summer. It is a good accompaniment for almost anything.

6–8 SERVINGS

1 small to medium cabbage, shredded
4 medium carrots, grated
6 scallions, finely sliced
$1/2$ cup mayonnaise
3 tablespoons white vinegar
2 tablespoons lemon juice
salt and pepper to taste

Combine the vegetables in a big bowl. Add the mayonnaise and the remaining ingredients. Mix very well and place the bowl in the refrigerator for at least 2 hours before serving. Serve cold.

Chinese Cabbage Salad

This salad makes a good appetizer for a relaxed lunch or brunch.

6–8 SERVINGS

1 head Chinese cabbage, sliced julienne style
2 large carrots, sliced julienne style
1 onion, thinly sliced
4 tangerines, peeled and separated into segments
2 apples, peeled and thinly sliced
$^1/_4$ pound goat cheese, crumbled

Vinaigrette

8 tablespoons walnut or hazelnut oil
2 tablespoons lemon juice
2 tablespoons aromatic and fruity vinegar (raspberry or similar flavor)
salt and pepper to taste
fresh chives, finely chopped

1. Place the vegetables and fruits in a deep salad bowl.

2. Mix all the dressing ingredients well in a small bowl. When you are ready to serve, add the crumbled goat cheese to the salad. Pour the dressing over the salad and toss it a few times to see that the vegetables and fruits are equally well coated. Serve immediately.

VALAMO CABBAGE SOUP

This soup can also be refrigerated and served cold.

6 SERVINGS

1 small white cabbage, thinly sliced
2 large potatoes, peeled and diced
2 medium onions, sliced
8 cups water
1 teaspoon paprika
$\frac{1}{2}$ teaspoon cumin
pinch cayenne pepper
salt to taste
1 (8-ounce) container plain yogurt or sour cream
fresh parsley, finely chopped, as garnish

1. Place the vegetables and water in a large soup kettle and bring to a boil. Lower the heat to medium and add the paprika, cumin, cayenne pepper, and salt. Stir a few times. Cover the pot and cook for about 30 minutes. Allow the soup to cool.

2. When the soup has cooled a bit, place it in a blender and whirl it for a minute or so until it is well mixed. Pour the creamy soup back into the kettle, add the yogurt or sour cream, and mix it well with a large spoon. Reheat the soup before serving, but do not bring it to a boil. Serve the soup hot and garnish the top of each serving with chopped parsley.

Kale Asian Style

4 SERVINGS

$1/2$ pound fresh kale
3 tablespoons vegetable oil
3 slices fresh ginger
3 garlic cloves, minced
sea salt to taste
1 teaspoon honey
1 tablespoon cider vinegar
6 tablespoons water or more as needed

1. Trim and discard the bottom inch at the base of the kale leaves or stalks. Cut the leaves in quarters lengthwise. Then cut them further into 2-inch lengths, and transfer the pieces to a large bowl. Toss with your hands, loosening the leaves and stems.

2. Heat a wok or large deep cast-iron skillet over high heat. Add the oil, swirling to coat the pan evenly.

3. Add the ginger, garlic, and salt to the heated oil and toss well. Add the kale and toss again. Lower the heat to medium and continue cooking until the kale begins to wilt. Stir continuously for 2–3 minutes.

4. Add the honey, vinegar, and water. Continue tossing and stirring until the kale is cooked and tender. Taste and adjust the seasonings as desired. If necessary, add a bit more water to prevent the kale from burning. When the kale is done, transfer it to a serving plate and serve as an accompaniment to a main course.

Broccoli and Tomato Casserole

This is a wonderful winter dish, and it should be served as a main course. It is a complete meal in itself.

1/3 cup olive oil
2 heads broccoli, sliced into florets and stem parts
6 medium tomatoes, peeled and sliced
1 cup fresh mushrooms, sliced
1 large onion, sliced
2 garlic cloves, minced
1/2 cup fresh basil, chopped
2 cups uncooked egg noodles (more if necessary)
3 eggs
1/2 cup milk
salt and pepper to taste
1/2 cup grated cheese
bread crumbs

1. Pour the oil into a large, deep skillet and add all the vegetables except the garlic. Sauté the vegetables over medium-low heat until tender, then add the garlic and basil. Stir well, turn off the heat, and cover the skillet.

2. Boil the noodles in salted water for about 8 minutes. Drain and coat with a bit of olive oil. Set aside.

3. Beat the eggs in a deep bowl, add the milk, salt and pepper, and half the grated cheese. Mix well.

4. Preheat the oven to 350°F. Thoroughly butter or oil a long baking dish; combine the vegetables and add with noodles, distributing them evenly. Pour the egg mixture on top. Sprinkle the rest of the grated cheese on top and then the bread crumbs. Bake for 30–40 minutes. Serve hot.

SAINT GERTRUDE BROCCOLI SALAD

Serve this salad as an appetizer during the harvest months, when tomatoes are at their best.

4–6 SERVINGS

1 large head (or 2 medium heads) broccoli
pinch salt
1 large bunch mesclun (tender salad greens)
6 medium tomatoes, peeled and diced
1 red onion, thinly sliced

Vinaigrette
4 tablespoons olive oil
3 tablespoons walnut oil
3 tablespoons wine vinegar
2 tablespoons lemon juice
$1/2$ teaspoon creamy mustard (without seeds)
salt and freshly ground pepper to taste

1. Put the broccoli in a container with cold water to cover for 1 hour or until you are ready to use it. Then carefully separate the florets and cut the top parts of the stem into thin slices. Discard the tough parts.

2. Place the broccoli in a saucepan. Add salted water to cover and boil over medium heat for 6–7 minutes. Drain immediately and rinse in cold water to preserve its freshness and color. Set aside.

3. Wash and dry the mesclun greens.

4. Just before serving, mix all the vegetables in a deep bowl. Prepare the vinaigrette by mixing the ingredients thoroughly in a small bowl; pour the vinaigrette over the vegetables. Toss the salad with care and be mindful to see that all the vegetables are well coated.

Broccoli au Gratin

This is a good accompaniment for egg, fish, and meat main courses.

6 SERVINGS

3 medium heads broccoli, trimmed
7 large potatoes, peeled
1 onion, sliced
2 tablespoons olive oil
5 garlic cloves, minced
1 pint heavy cream
salt and pepper to taste
dash nutmeg
$1/2$ cup grated cheese of your preference

1. Cook the broccoli and potatoes in boiling water until they are tender. Drain them, chop them coarsely, and mash them.

2. Place the sliced onion in a skillet, pour in olive oil, and sauté over medium-low heat for 1–2 minutes. Then add the garlic, stir well, and withdraw the skillet from the heat.

3. Preheat the oven to 350°F. Place the mashed broccoli and potatoes in a deep bowl. Add the onion and garlic mixture, cream, salt and pepper, and nutmeg. Mix all the ingredients well.

4. Thoroughly butter a long, flat ovenproof dish and generously sprinkle half of the grated cheese over the buttered surface. Closely pack the creamy vegetable mixture into the dish and smooth the top evenly. Sprinkle the remaining grated cheese over the entire top and bake the casserole for approximately 30 minutes. Serve hot.

Broccoli and Pasta San Giorgio

4 SERVINGS

$1/2$ pound fresh broccoli
$1/3$ cup plus 2 tablespoons olive oil
2 cups rotini pasta (or other pasta of your preference)
$1/3$ cup fresh basil
6 garlic cloves, peeled
pepper to taste
grated Romano cheese for the table

1. Cut the broccoli into florets. Discard the rest. Place the broccoli in a saucepan of salted boiling water. Add 2 tablespoons olive oil. After 5 minutes, add the pasta and continue cooking over medium heat for about 10 minutes or until pasta is tender but al dente. Stir occasionally.

2. While the broccoli and pasta are cooking, prepare the sauce by placing the basil and garlic in a food processor or blender and adding $1/3$ cup olive oil and pepper. Whirl for a minute or two until the sauce acquires an even consistency. Add more oil if necessary.

3. When the broccoli and pasta are ready, drain and place back in the pan, add the basil-garlic sauce, and mix with care. Serve hot, accompanied by grated cheese at the table.

BROCCOLI FLANS

This dish can be served as a main course accompanied by potatoes or other vegetables. It also makes a wonderful appetizer.

6–8 SERVINGS

3 medium heads broccoli, trimmed
pinch salt
2 tablespoons butter
4 teaspoons cornstarch
2 cups milk
salt and pepper to taste
dash nutmeg
4 large eggs

1. Cut the broccoli into florets and the stems into 1-inch slices. Place them in a saucepan with salted water and bring to a boil. Cover the pan and cook for about 20 minutes. Drain and then puree it in a food processor or blender. Set aside.

2. Prepare the béchamel sauce by melting the butter in a saucepan over medium-low heat. Add the cornstarch and stir continuously with a whisk. Add the milk gradually. Add salt and pepper to taste and a dash of nutmeg and continue stirring. When the sauce begins to boil, reduce the heat to low and continue cooking slowly until it thickens.

3. Preheat the oven to 350°F. In a deep bowl, beat 4 eggs well, then add the pureed broccoli and the béchamel sauce. Mix all the ingredients thoroughly.

4. Place the broccoli mixture in six or eight well-buttered ovenproof ramekins (small bowls or dishes). Place the ramekins in a long, flat metal pan; add water to cover halfway up the sides of the ramekins. Bake for 30 minutes. When the flans are done (when a thin knife is inserted in the center and comes out clean), unmold carefully and serve hot.

Brussels Sprouts Provençal Style

This dish can be served as an appetizer or as an accompaniment for eggs, fish, or meat.

6–8 SERVINGS

1 pound brussels sprouts, trimmed
4 tablespoons olive oil, plus more if needed
2 large onions, chopped
4 garlic cloves, minced
5 tomatoes, peeled and chopped
1 bay leaf
pinch Provençal herbs (thyme, rosemary, basil)
1 (6-ounce) can pitted black olives, drained
salt and pepper to taste

1. Boil the brussels sprouts in salted water for about 20 minutes. Drain.

2. Pour the olive oil into a heavy casserole (cast-iron, if possible). Add the rest of the ingredients. Cover the casserole and cook the vegetables over low heat for 25–30 minutes. Stir from time to time and watch that nothing sticks to the bottom.

3. After 30 minutes, add the cooked brussels sprouts, stir well, and cover the casserole again. Continue cooking over low heat for 8–10 minutes. Remove the bay leaf, adjust the seasonings as wanted, and serve immediately.

BRUSSELS SPROUTS WITH ONIONS

Serve as an accompaniment for meat or fish or a vegetarian main dish. This is a special treat when brussels sprouts are in season.

4–6 SERVINGS

4 tablespoons olive oil
5 medium onions, sliced
1 pound brussels sprouts, trimmed
salt and pepper to taste
$1^{1}/_{2}$ cups water, plus more if needed

1. Pour the olive oil into a good-size cast-iron pot or skillet. Add the sliced onions and sauté lightly over medium-low heat for 1–2 minutes.

2. Reduce the heat to low, add the brussels sprouts and salt and pepper, and cover with water. Cover the pot and cook slowly for 75–90 minutes. Check from time to time to see that the vegetables don't burn at the bottom. The vegetables will develop a strong flavor because of the onions and they will be ready when all the water is absorbed. Serve hot.

Thanksgiving Brussels Sprouts

This goes nicely as an accompaniment to a main course.

4–6 SERVINGS

2 cups or 1 (15-ounce) jar drained cocktail onions
2 cups baby carrots
2 cups small brussels sprouts, trimmed
salt to taste
$1/2$ cup maple syrup
1 tablespoon mustard
pepper to taste

1. Peel the small onions if fresh. Wash the baby carrots.

2. Put the brussels sprouts and the carrots in a good-size saucepan; add salted water to cover and bring to a boil. Cover the saucepan and cook over medium heat for 10 minutes. Add the small onions and cook for another 5 minutes. Drain the vegetables thoroughly.

3. Into an empty saucepan pour the maple syrup and add the mustard. Mix well. Add the drained vegetables, sprinkle on some pepper, and cook over medium-low heat until most of the maple syrup is absorbed by the vegetables. Stir frequently so the vegetables do not burn at the bottom. Serve hot.

Sister Placid's Cauliflower and Garlic Soup

6–8 SERVINGS

8 cups vegetable stock or water
2 large potatoes, peeled and diced
1 large head cauliflower
7 tablespoons olive oil
salt and freshly ground pepper to taste
1 head garlic
6–8 tablespoons olive oil as garnish

1. Place vegetable stock or water in a large soup pot. If water is used instead of stock, add a pinch of salt. Add the diced potatoes and bring to a quick boil for 4–5 minutes. Remove from heat and set aside.

2. Preheat the oven to 350°F. Cut the cauliflower into small pieces, toss with 5 tablespoons olive oil and salt and pepper. Place in a good-size baking pan, in a single layer, and bake for about 30 minutes.

3. In the meantime, peel the garlic cloves and toss them in the remaining 2 tablespoons olive oil. Wrap them in foil and place them in the oven alongside the pan of cauliflower for about 20 minutes.

4. While the vegetables are roasting, puree the potatoes and stock in a blender. Pour the puree back into the soup pot. Add the cooked cauliflower and garlic cloves to the soup and bring to a quick boil. Reduce the heat and simmer for 10–15 minutes.

5. Remove the soup from the stove and allow it to cool. Then pass it through a blender in small batches. Check the seasonings, and if need be, add salt and pepper. Serve the soup hot, or chill it for a couple of hours and serve it cold during the hot weather months. Add a tablespoon of olive oil at the center of each serving as garnish.

Cauliflower with Roquefort Sauce

4 SERVINGS

1 head cauliflower
3 shallots (or medium onions), minced
2 tablespoons butter
4 ounces Roquefort cheese, crumbled
4 ounces crème fraîche or sour cream
salt and pepper to taste
fresh parsley, finely chopped, as garnish

1. Slice and separate the cauliflower into florets. Make sure that each remains whole and intact. Cook the cauliflower in the top of a double boiler, the bottom part of which contains several cups of water. Cover the pot. Cook over medium heat for about 15 minutes.

2. While the cauliflower is cooking, prepare the sauce by lightly sautéing the shallots in butter for about 2 minutes. Immediately add the crumbled cheese and continue cooking for another 2 minutes, stirring continuously while the cheese melts. Add the crème fraîche and salt and pepper and continue stirring for another 1–2 minutes, until the sauce achieves an even consistency.

3. Drain the cauliflower and place it in a warm serving dish. While it is hot, pour the sauce over it and sprinkle the chopped parsley on the top as garnish. Serve hot.

Cauliflower Italian Style

4 SERVINGS

1 large cauliflower with its tender green leaves
salt and cayenne pepper to taste
6 tablespoons lemon juice
4 teaspoons butter
5 tablespoons cream or half-and-half
garlic powder to taste

1. Place the whole cauliflower intact, with its tender leaves, in a good-size saucepan filled with plenty of water. Cover the pan and bring the water to a boil. Cook for 10 minutes, watching that the cauliflower remains firm. Drain the cauliflower and place it in a container filled with cold water. Drain again.

2. With great care, detach the florets and the individual leaves from the main trunk, making sure they remain firm and intact. Place them in a saucepan filled with boiling water, add salt and cayenne pepper and the lemon juice. Boil for 5 minutes. Drain the cauliflower and let cold water run over it. Drain again.

3. Melt the butter in a good-size deep skillet over medium-low heat. Add the cauliflower florets and leaves. Cover the skillet for 2 minutes; then add the cream and sprinkle a small amount of garlic powder over the dish. Stir. Cover the skillet and continue cooking over medium-low heat for 3 more minutes. Serve hot.

CAULIFLOWER WITH OLIVES PROVENÇAL STYLE

*This is a good accompaniment for almost any main course.
It goes especially well with egg dishes such as a soufflé.*

4–6 SERVINGS

4 tablespoons olive oil
2 onions, sliced
2 garlic cloves, minced
1 large cauliflower, cut into florets
1 (6-ounce) can pitted black olives, drained
$^1/_2$ cup water
$^1/_3$ cup dry white wine
salt and pepper to taste
pinch cumin

1. Pour the olive oil into a heavy saucepan (cast-iron if possible). Heat the oil at medium-low and add the onions. Sauté for 2 minutes. Reduce the heat to low and add the garlic, cauliflower, drained olives, water, and white wine. Add the salt and pepper and cumin. Stir gently a few times and cover the saucepan. Cook over low heat for about 1 hour. Check from time to time whether more water is needed. You can also add more wine if you prefer.

2. After 1 hour, turn off the heat and keep the vegetables hot until you are ready to serve.

CAULIFLOWER DIP

You may add other fresh vegetables, such as radishes, cherry tomatoes, and carrot sticks, to the cauliflower.

6 SERVINGS

1 large head cauliflower
salt to taste

Dip Sauce Piquant
1 (8-ounce) container low-fat sour cream
3 tablespoons mayonnaise
1 tablespoon ketchup
1 small onion, minced
$1/2$ teaspoon Tabasco sauce
1 tablespoon lemon juice
dash paprika
1 teaspoon Worcestershire sauce

Sweet Herb and Egg Dip Sauce
1 (8-ounce) container low-fat yogurt
3 tablespoons mayonnaise
2 tablespoons mustard
1 tablespoon lemon juice
1 hard-boiled egg, finely chopped
handful fresh parsley, finely minced
handful scallions, finely minced
handful fresh cilantro, finely minced

1. Slice the cauliflower carefully into florets. Place them in a saucepan with water to cover. Add salt and bring to a quick boil. Cover the pot and boil for exactly 1 minute. Drain immediately and rinse in very cold water. Set aside until the florets are completely dry. Serve in a dish with one of the two sauces on the side.

2. To make either sauce, mix all ingredients well until a smooth consistency is achieved. Check the seasonings and add salt if needed.

CARROTS & PARSNIPS

(Daucus carota and Pastinaca sativa)

The carrot, a humble root vegetable, had its origin in the country that today is called Afghanistan. Though already known in ancient times by the Romans and Greeks, the Germans and the Slavs, the carrot received very little notice in history. For instance, it is not mentioned among the ninety eatable plants in the capitulary called De Villis, which registered the names of the plants in the gardens of the Emperor Charlemagne.

Around the sixteenth century, the carrot all of a sudden began to surface and receive appreciation, thanks to a certain experiment in Holland that changed its light brown color to orange, the vegetable thus receiving the name long orange carrot. After that its cultivation expanded throughout Europe, the Americas, and around the world, and it became one of the most popular vegetables at the table.

In olden times, the carrot, like other vegetables, was thought to give protection against certain illnesses. In particular, it was strongly recommended to fight stomach and intestinal problems. To this can be added today's conviction that carrots are very useful in the prevention of cancer. Carrots are a source of vitamins A, B, and C and are even more important as a source of carotene, a great aid to the skin and the eyes. Parsnips are related to the carrot family; therefore, a recipe for parsnips is included in this section.

CARROT TIMBALES

The timbales can be served hot or cold, as an appetizer, or as an accompaniment to a main dish.

6 SERVINGS

8 carrots, sliced
1¹/₂ tablespoons butter
3 eggs
1 cup milk
salt and pepper to taste
1¹/₂ tablespoons brown sugar

1. Add water to a good-size casserole, and bring to a boil. Add the sliced carrots. Cook for 25–30 minutes, until tender when pierced with a fork. Drain and then process in a food processor until they turn into a creamy puree.

2. Melt the butter in a large casserole and add the pureed carrots. Cook over low heat for a few minutes, stirring continuously so the puree does not burn at the bottom. After 3–5 minutes, remove the casserole from the stove and let it cool for a while.

3. Preheat the oven to 350°F. Place the eggs, milk, seasoning, and brown sugar in a blender, and mix thoroughly. Pour this mixture gradually into the casserole with the pureed carrots, whisking the mixture with the other hand at the same time.

4. Thoroughly butter six small ramekins. Divide the carrot mixture among them.

5. Put the ramekins in a long roasting pan and fill it with water up to half the height of the ramekins. Bake the timbales for 40–45 minutes until they are firm and smooth. Add some water to the pan during the cooking, if necessary, so that it is never dry.

6. When the timbales are done, remove them carefully from the water bath and let them cool for 1 minute before taking them out of their molds. Place a small plate on top of each ramekin and then quickly turn it upside down. Lift the ramekin off very gently so as to preserve the timbale intact.

CARROT FANTASY

This is a good accompaniment to a main course.

6 SERVINGS

5 tablespoons vegetable oil
1 large onion, thinly sliced
3 celery stalks, sliced
8 carrots, cut into thin slices 3 inches long, and then again
    in 4 parts lengthwise
1 bouillon cube (flavor of your choice)
1 cup water, plus more if necessary
2 tablespoons cornstarch
$^1/_3$ cup half-and-half or milk
salt and pepper to taste

1. Pour the oil into a deep heavy pot. Add the sliced onion and celery. Sauté for several minutes until they become tender.

2. Add the carrot sticks, bouillon cube, and water. Cover the pot and bring to a boil. Lower the heat to medium-low for 10 minutes, until the water is absorbed. Watch that the vegetables do not burn at the bottom.

3. Sprinkle the cornstarch over the vegetables, add the half-and-half or milk and salt and pepper, and continue cooking, stirring constantly, for 6–8 minutes, until the carrots are bathed in a smooth cream. Serve hot.

Carrot Juice

This drink makes a delicious appetizer with a cool summer lunch.

4 SERVINGS

1 pound fresh carrots
$1/2$ pound fresh tomatoes
$1/2$ cup fresh orange juice
2 tablespoons lemon juice
1 tablespoon fresh parsley or chervil, finely chopped

1. Wash and clean the carrots well. Slice them and pass them through a juice extractor.

2. Wash and clean the tomatoes well. Slice them into quarters and pass them through a juice extractor.

3. Mix the two juices together and add the orange juice, lemon juice, and chopped parsley or chervil. Stir and mix well. Chill in the refrigerator for 1–2 hours before serving.

Orange-Flavored Baby Carrots

This is delicious as an accompaniment to a main course. On festive occasions you could add pearl onions to the baby carrots. They could be frozen or from a can if there is no time to peel fresh ones.

6 SERVINGS

1 pound baby carrots, cleaned, trimmed, and peeled
2^1/$_2$ cups orange juice, plus more if needed
2 tablespoons mustard
pinch salt
pepper to taste
3 tablespoons butter
4 tablespoons brown sugar or honey
2 tablespoons fresh tarragon, finely chopped
   (or 1 teaspoon dried)

1. Place the carrots in a saucepan. Add the orange juice, mustard, and salt. Cover the saucepan and cook over medium-low heat until all the liquid is absorbed. Stir from time to time. At the end of the cooking, add pepper to taste and mix well.

2. Preheat the oven to 300°F. Melt the butter in a large skillet, add the carrots, brown sugar or honey, and tarragon. Mix well and cook over low heat for about 2 minutes, stirring frequently.

3. Thoroughly butter a baking dish with a cover, place the carrots in it, and sprinkle some additional brown sugar on top. Cook in the oven for 15 minutes and serve hot.

COLD CARROT SALAD

This is an excellent appetizer for lunch or supper. To present it at the table in an attractive way, place some fresh lettuce leaves on each serving dish and put the carrots on top. This salad can also be accompanied by sliced tomatoes and hard-boiled eggs sliced in half.

8 large carrots, sliced julienne style
4 tablespoons lemon juice
10 mint leaves, finely chopped and shredded
1 small onion, diced
$1/2$ cup golden raisins
$1/3$ cup mayonnaise
$1/2$ teaspoon French mustard (Dijon or other)
salt and pepper to taste

1. Place the carrots in a deep bowl. Add the lemon juice and mix well. Refrigerate for a few hours until almost time to serve.

2. Just before serving, take the bowl from the refrigerator and add the finely shredded mint leaves, diced onion, raisins, mayonnaise, mustard, and salt and pepper, and mix well. Serve immediately, for this salad should always be served cold.

Carrots Provençal Style

4–6 SERVINGS

1 pound carrots
6 tablespoons olive oil
3 garlic cloves, minced
1/4 cup fresh parsley, minced
pinch thyme
pinch rosemary
1 bay leaf
1 1/2 cups dry white wine
salt and pepper to taste

1. Cut the carrots into round, thin slices. Place them in a deep cast-iron frying pan or saucepan. Pour in the olive oil and cook over medium-low heat for about 3 minutes. Stir frequently.

2. Add the garlic, parsley, and the other herbs. Add the wine and salt and pepper. Cover the pan and cook for 15–20 minutes, until all the liquid evaporates. Stir from time to time and watch that the carrots do not burn on the bottom. Remove the bay leaf and serve hot.

PARSNIP CHOWDER

4–6 SERVINGS

5 tablespoons butter
1 small onion, chopped
2 shallots, chopped
2 cups fresh mushrooms, chopped
4 medium parsnips, peeled and chopped
2 cups water
3 cups milk, whole or low-fat
$^1/_2$ cup cracker crumbs
salt and pepper to taste
fresh parsley, finely chopped, as garnish

1. Melt 3 tablespoons butter in a saucepan. Add the onion, shallots, and mushrooms and cook over low heat for 4–5 minutes, stirring continuously.

2. Add the parsnips and water and bring to a quick boil. Reduce the heat to medium-low, cover, and cook for about 20 minutes, until the parsnips are done. (Add more water, if necessary.)

3. Add the milk and mix. When the soup is near boiling, reduce the heat to low and add the remaining 2 tablespoons butter, cracker crumbs, and salt and pepper, mix well. Serve the chowder hot and sprinkle some chopped parsley on top as garnish.

Celery & Celery Root

(Apium graveolens)

The celery and its cousin the celery root, sometimes called celeriac (*céleri-rave* in French), are originally members of the same plant family. It is believed that their provenance is found in the Mediterranean Basin. Both celeries grow well in a terrain where there is an abundance of water and sun. The soil, of course, needs to be deep and rich in compost and other types of natural fertilizers. Here in our small monastery we usually import the seeds of the celery root from France, where they cultivate some excellent varieties.

In France the celery root is considered a légume gourmand, a gourmet type of vegetable, hence its extensive cultivation in the French soil and the deep appreciation of it at the table. The celery root is beginning to gain the interest of both gardeners and restaurateurs in this country, as one occasionally sees it on the menus of some of the best restaurants. It is also beginning to appear in some of the better markets. This past summer I was delighted to discover celery root in a nearby market in Great Barrington, Massachusetts, that specializes in gourmet products. It is clear the word is getting around.

Both types of celeries are commonly used here at the monastic table. They can be eaten raw or cooked, alone or combined with other vegetables. It is up to the good art and taste of the ingenious cook how to use and prepare them properly.

CELERY ROOT RÉMOULADE

Serve the celery roots as an appetizer. You may wish to place them on top of lettuce leaves.

4 SERVINGS

4 medium celery roots, peeled and sliced julienne style
4 tablespoons lemon juice

Rémoulade Sauce
1 egg yolk
2 tablespoons French mustard (a strong one, with seeds)
1/2 cup olive oil
1 tablespoon tarragon-scented (or other) vinegar
salt and pepper to taste

1. Cook the celery roots for about 1 minute in boiling water and then drain them completely. Place them in a deep bowl. Add the lemon juice, mix well, and refrigerate for at least 2 hours or until almost ready to serve.

2. Place the egg yolk in a deep bowl and add the mustard. Then add the oil gradually as you whisk the mixture with an electric mixer. Add the vinegar and salt and pepper and whisk some more until the sauce achieves an even consistency. Keep in the refrigerator until needed.

3. When you are ready to serve, add the celery roots to the sauce and mix thoroughly. Serve cold.

Celery Root Mousseline

6–8 SERVINGS

2 pounds potatoes
1 pound celery roots
pinch salt
4 tablespoons butter
1 (8-ounce) container crème fraîche or heavy cream
pinch fresh tarragon, finely chopped
salt and pepper to taste

1. Wash the potatoes and the celery roots. Pull the celery roots apart and slice both vegetables into chunks.

2. Fill a large saucepan with water and add salt. Boil the potatoes for about 12 minutes. Add the celery roots and continue boiling for another 10–12 minutes. Drain thoroughly.

3. Mash the vegetables or pass them through a food mill or processor. Add the butter, crème fraîche, tarragon, and salt and pepper and mix until the mousseline achieves an even consistency.

4. Butter a good-size Pyrex dish thoroughly. Spread the mousseline evenly in the dish and place it in a 200°F oven to keep it warm until time to serve.

STUFFED CELERY STALKS GRATINÉE

This can be served as an appetizer or as an accompaniment to a main course. It goes well with fish.

4–6 SERVINGS

2 tablespoons butter
1 bunch celery, trimmed and stalks cut in half
$1/3$ cup dry white wine, plus more if needed
salt
3 tablespoons olive oil
3 tomatoes, peeled, seeded, and sliced
2 garlic cloves, minced
10 black olives, pitted and finely chopped
8 fresh basil leaves, finely chopped, or 2 teaspoons
    dried basil
pepper
grated Parmesan cheese, or cheese of your choice

1. Melt the butter in a large, deep skillet and add the celery stalks, wine, and a pinch of salt. Cover the skillet and cook over low heat for 15 minutes. After the first 7 minutes turn the stalks over, cover the pot, and continue cooking for the remaining time.

2. While the celery is cooking, prepare the stuffing: Pour the oil into a medium skillet or saucepan, add the tomato slices, garlic, olives, basil, and salt and pepper to taste, and cook over low heat for about 5 minutes. Stir continuously.

3. Preheat the oven to 350°F. Thoroughly butter a long ovenproof dish. Put the stalks in the dish. Using a tablespoon, fill the stalks with the tomato-olive stuffing to the top. Cover the top of each with grated cheese.

4. Place the dish in the oven for 20–25 minutes. Serve the stuffed celery hot.

Celery and Carrots with Honey and Mustard

This dish makes an attractive accompaniment to a main course.

4 SERVINGS

8 celery stalks, sliced
4 long thin carrots, sliced
1 cup orange juice
1 cup water, plus more if needed
2 shallots, finely chopped
1 tablespoon mustard
3 tablespoons honey
salt and pepper to taste

1. Place the sliced celery stalks and carrots in a saucepan and add the orange juice and water. Bring to a boil and then reduce the heat to medium-low. Cover the saucepan and cook slowly until almost all the liquid evaporates. Stir occasionally.
2. Add the shallots, mustard, honey, and salt and pepper and mix well. Cover the pot and continue cooking for 1–2 minutes, being careful not to burn the bottom. Stir well and serve hot.

CORN

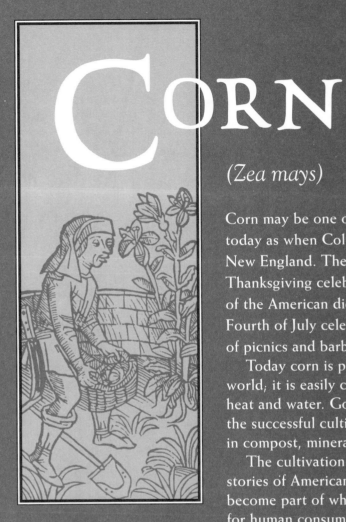

(Zea mays)

Corn may be one of the quintessentially American foods, as popular today as when Columbus came to the Americas and the Pilgrims settled in New England. The history books tell us that corn was served at that first Thanksgiving celebration back in 1621, and it has been a standard feature of the American diet ever since. It is almost impossible for us to think of a Fourth of July celebration that does not include fresh corn in the millions of picnics and barbecues across the country.

Today corn is popular not only across the Americas but throughout the world; it is easily cultivated wherever the climate provides good doses of heat and water. Good, fertile soil and excellent seeds are also essential to the successful cultivation of corn. The soil should be well drained and rich in compost, minerals, and nitrogen.

The cultivation of corn as a grain has become one of the great success stories of American agriculture. Entire regions of the western states have become part of what is today called the Corn Belt. Corn is grown not only for human consumption but primarily, and perhaps more importantly, as animal feed. From a nutritional point of view, corn may be considered of more value to the feeding of livestock than the feeding of humans. Corn is low in protein and vitamin B but rich in starch, providing many uses for manufacturers, laundry industries, and housewives throughout the years.

Corn, in the kitchen and at the table, is principally a summer crop. Following the tradition of their ancestors, the local farmers where I live remind me every year that corn should be shucked at the last moment, just before cooking. If it is to be eaten on the cob, it should be boiled for 3–4 minutes maximum and eaten immediately after. Corn and its derivative, cornmeal, are consumed in some cultures as a food staple similar to bread: polenta in Italy, grits in the southern United States, tortillas in Mexico, for example. Basically, corn is a humble grain that lends itself to an infinite variety of uses.

Saint Lawrence Corn Soup

4–6 SERVINGS

6 tablespoons vegetable oil
2 onions, sliced
2 garlic cloves, minced
3 celery stalks, thinly sliced
7 cups water, plus more if needed
1 bouillon cube (flavor of your choice)
1 red pepper, diced
1 potato, cut into cubes
corn kernels from 5 ears, or 1 (8-ounce) package frozen corn
salt and pepper to taste
fresh cilantro (or parsley), chopped, as garnish

1. Pour the oil into a soup pot. Add the onions, garlic, and celery and sauté over low heat for about 2 minutes, until the onions begin to turn color.

2. Add the water and bouillon cube and bring the water to a boil. Add the red pepper, potato, corn kernels, and salt and pepper. Cover the pot and cook for about 20 minutes over medium-low heat. Stir the soup several times, adjust the seasonings as needed, and simmer for another 10 minutes. Serve the soup hot, topping each serving with chopped cilantro or parsley as garnish.

Saint Martin Corn Soufflé

This dish should be served as a main course. It could be accompanied by another cooked vegetable in season.

4–6 SERVINGS

1 onion
1 teaspoon plus 3 tablespoons butter
3 tablespoons cornstarch
1 cup milk
$1/2$ cup shredded sharp Cheddar cheese
5 egg yolks
2 cups well-drained cooked corn
salt and pepper to taste
5 egg whites, beaten stiff
grated Parmesan cheese

1. Chop the onion coarsely and sauté in 1 teaspoon butter over low heat for about 2 minutes. Set aside.

2. Preheat the oven to 350°F.

3. Melt 3 tablespoons of butter in a small casserole. Dissolve the cornstarch in the milk and then pour the mixture, a little at a time, into the melting butter. Stir continuously until the sauce achieves a thick consistency. Turn off the heat. Add the shredded cheese and stir well. Allow the mixture to cool for a few minutes.

4. Beat the egg yolks in a deep bowl, add the cheese mixture, and stir well. Add the cooked corn and the sautéed onion. Add salt and pepper. Stir thoroughly. Add the beaten egg whites and carefully fold them into the mixture.

5. Thoroughly butter a soufflé dish and sprinkle grated cheese over the buttered surface. Pour the egg and corn mixture into it with care. Bake for 30–40 minutes. The soufflé is ready when the top gets brown and begins to puff at the center. It should be served immediately after it comes out of the oven.

SAINT MARTHA CORN CASSEROLE

This is an ideal dish to serve around the end of July or early August, when the new corn begins to arrive. In the monastery we begin to serve new corn around July 29, the feast of Saint Martha, hence the name given to the recipe.

6–8 SERVINGS

7 ears new corn
4 tablespoons olive or other oil
1 large onion, thinly sliced
4 large tomatoes, peeled and chopped
3 garlic cloves, minced
fresh parsley, finely chopped, to taste
salt and pepper to taste
2 medium yellow squash, cut into small chunks
2 medium zucchini, cut into small chunks
4 tablespoons water
$1/2$ cup grated Cheddar cheese

1. Separate the kernels from the ears of corn with a long, sharp knife. Place them immediately in salted boiling water for 2–3 minutes. Drain and set them aside.

2. Pour the oil into a large, heavy saucepan and add the onion, tomatoes, garlic, parsley, and salt and pepper. Cook over medium-low heat for about 3 minutes, until the mixture begins to turn into a sauce. Stir occasionally.

3. Preheat the oven to 350°F. Add the corn, squash, and zucchini to the onion-tomato sauce and mix well. Cover the saucepan, reduce the heat to low, and continue cooking for 4–5 minutes. Stir occasionally. Add the water to increase the sauce.

4. Thoroughly butter an ovenproof casserole dish and spoon the vegetable mixture into it. Cover the top with the grated cheese and bake for about 20 minutes, until the cheese turns bubbly and melts. Serve hot.

FRESH CORN POLENTA

4 SERVINGS

2 cups corn kernels (about 4 ears of new corn)
1 onion, diced
2 tablespoons olive oil
3 cups water
1 cup coarse or fine-grained polenta (cornmeal)
pinch salt
freshly ground pepper to taste
3 tablespoons butter
6 tablespoons grated Parmesan cheese
crushed fresh rosemary leaves

1. Place the corn kernels in a saucepan. Add water to cover and boil for 5 minutes, then drain and set aside.

2. Sauté the onion in the olive oil over medium-low heat for 2–3 minutes. Set aside.

3. Bring the water to a boil in a good-size saucepan and gradually add the polenta and salt. Stir continuously until the mixture thickens, about 15 minutes. Add the corn and the onion and continue cooking and stirring constantly until the polenta and all elements are thoroughly blended.

4. During the last minutes of cooking, add the pepper, butter, grated cheese, and rosemary. Mix well and serve hot. The polenta may be served on a large preheated platter, in a bowl, or on individual dishes. It can also be kept warm in a preheated oven until ready to serve.

Corn-Stuffed Tomatoes

This is an excellent dish to serve as a main course during the late summer months or early fall, when there is an abundance of corn and tomatoes from the garden.

6 SERVINGS

6 large firm ripe tomatoes
2 tablespoons olive oil
1 onion, diced
3 eggs
$1/2$ cup milk
2 cups cooked corn kernels (scraped from the ears)
$1/3$ cup grated cheese (your favorite)
finely chopped parsley
1 teaspoon dried thyme (or 3 teaspoons fresh)
6 rosemary leaves, crushed
a few basil leaves, chopped
salt and pepper to taste

1. Cut off the top end of the tomatoes and scoop out the insides. (Save for a sauce or discard.)

2. Pour the oil into a skillet and sauté the onion for 4–5 minutes maximum. Preheat the oven to 300°F.

3. Beat the eggs in a deep bowl, add the milk, and beat some more. Add the corn kernels, grated cheese, onion, herbs, and salt and pepper and mix all these ingredients well.

4. Butter a baking dish thoroughly and place the tomatoes in the dish next to one another. Fill each one to the top with the egg-corn mixture. Sprinkle more grated cheese on each tomato. Bake for 45 minutes. Serve hot.

COLD CORN SALAD

This salad can be served as an appetizer during the summer months, when fresh new corn is available.

4 ears new corn
1 red pepper, diced
1 (6-ounce) can tuna fish, well drained and chopped
1 (6-ounce) can pitted black olives, well drained
1 red onion, chopped
4 hard-boiled eggs, chopped
chopped parsley to taste

Vinaigrette
6 tablespoons olive oil
3 tablespoons vinegar
salt and pepper to taste

1. Cook the corn ears in salted boiling water for about 5 minutes. Drain them and then slice the kernels off the cobs. Place the kernels in a deep salad bowl. Add the diced pepper and the tuna.

2. Slice the black olives in half and add them to the bowl. Add the onion and hard-boiled eggs. Mix well and place in the refrigerator for at least 2 hours before serving.

3. Just before serving, add the chopped parsley to the salad mixture. Combine all the vinaigrette ingredients well in a small bowl, and pour the dressing over the salad. Toss the salad and serve it cold.

CUCUMBERS

(Cucumis sativus)

Cucumber is one of the plants mentioned in the Bible. We have references to it in the Old Testament in the Book of Numbers, in the Prophet Isaiah, and others. From the Old Testament we know that the cucumber was cultivated in ancient Egypt, and from there its cultivation expanded to Rome and other Mediterranean countries, including present-day Israel. This is not surprising since the countries of the Mediterranean Basin offer the proper climate for its cultivation. There are some theories among botanists that the cucumber was also known in ancient India and might have originated at the foot of the Himalayas. Whether or not that theory has any basis, the cucumber is popular today in India, as well as in China.

There are different varieties in the cucumber family, and many farmers and gardeners try to cultivate at least two or three types in their gardens. Such is the case in our monastery garden here in Millbrook. Among the several varieties are three that we cultivate assiduously every year, making different uses of them. The first is the small pickling variety called cornichon in French; the second variety is the longer common cucumber grown especially for use in salads; the third is a Middle Eastern type, perfect for making cold cucumber soup during hot summer months.

The cucumber in general is a vegetable of low nutritional content, and some people find it difficult to digest. However, the taste is so refreshing that it can be difficult to resist, especially during the hot weather months. The cucumber is also well known for enhancing and preserving beautiful skin. European cosmetologists and dermatologists often recommend the cosmetic use and consumption of cucumbers to protect the skin.

Baked Cucumbers with Cheese

This dish can be served as an appetizer or as an accompaniment to a main dish (half a cucumber per person).

4 SERVINGS

2 large cucumbers, peeled
$^1/_2$ (8-ounce) container low-fat sour cream
$^1/_2$ cup grated Gouda (or Gruyère) cheese
pinch powdered ginger
pinch nutmeg
salt and pepper to taste
butter as needed

1. Preheat the oven to 300°F. Carefully slice the cucumbers in half lengthwise, and with a small knife remove the seeds with great care. Place the cucumbers in a buttered baking dish.

2. In a bowl mix the sour cream, grated cheese, ginger, nutmeg, and salt and pepper until the mixture reaches an even, creamy consistency. (Add more sour cream or cheese if needed.) Spread this mixture evenly on the top of the sliced cucumbers and place small pieces of butter on the top.

3. Place the baking dish in the oven and bake for 15–20 minutes. When the cheese begins to turn slightly brown, the cucumbers are ready to be served.

Cold Cucumber Soup

This is an excellent appetizer for a good dinner during the hot months of summer.

6 SERVINGS

3 large cucumbers, peeled, sliced, and seeded
1 leek, white part only, sliced
6 cups water, plus more if needed
pinch saffron
pinch cayenne pepper
a few sprigs fresh chervil, chopped
salt and pepper to taste
juice of 1 lemon
1 (8-ounce) container plain yogurt
fresh chervil, finely chopped, as garnish

1. Place the cucumbers, leek, water, saffron, cayenne pepper, chervil, salt and pepper, and lemon juice in a good-size pot. Bring water to a boil, then lower the heat to medium-low and cook slowly for 15–20 minutes. Remove the pot from the heat and allow the soup to cool.

2. Whirl the soup in a blender or food processor. Pour it into a large bowl or pot, add the yogurt, and mix well by hand. Check the seasonings and refrigerate for several hours. Serve cold, topping each serving with chopped chervil.

CUCUMBERS STUFFED WITH TUNA

This is a good dish to serve for lunch or brunch.

4 SERVINGS

4 tomatoes, peeled and seeded, plus 1 sliced for garnish
2 shallots, minced
5 sprigs parsley, chopped
2 tablespoons butter
1 (5-ounce) can tuna, drained and finely chopped
salt and pepper to taste
2 medium cucumbers, peeled and seeded
grated cheese (optional)
olives, for garnish

1. Place the tomatoes, shallots, and parsley in a food processor and whirl into a sauce of smooth consistency. Melt the butter in a deep skillet. Pour the sauce into the skillet, add the tuna and salt and pepper, and cook over medium-low heat for 7–8 minutes. Stir frequently. After the sauce is cooked, set it aside.

2. Carefully slice the cucumbers in half lengthwise and split them at the center, removing all the seeds.

3. Preheat the oven to 300°F. Thoroughly butter an ovenproof dish. Place the cucumbers in it, and fill the centers with the tomato-tuna mixture. Sprinkle the grated cheese on top and place the stuffed cucumbers in the oven for 20–25 minutes. Serve warm, accompanied by tomato slices and a few olives as a garnish on each plate.

EGGPLANTS

(Solanum melongena)

Like the tomato, the eggplant is actually a fruit. In the Middle Ages, it was called Mala insana, which is to say "bad apple" or "crazy apple." Unfortunately, those ill-reputed names remained in vogue in Europe almost until the fifteenth century. Several scientists of the period, such as Leonardo Fuchsius and even Saint Hildegarde of Bingen, contributed to the poor reputation of the eggplant. Saint Hildegard, for instance, counseled that one should limit the eggplant strictly to therapeutic uses. She recommended it as a remedy for epilepsy.

While the eggplant had a hard time getting vindicated, it literally took centuries for it to be appreciated. Its reputation in Asian countries such as China, Japan, India, and Iran was always excellent. That is no surprise, since it seems certain that the eggplant's provenance was the Asian continent. Gradually, in the nineteenth century, the eggplant began taking a place of importance in certain areas of the Mediterranean: in southern Europe—in places such as Italy; France's Provence region; and Spain, where it was said to have been introduced by the Moors. The eggplant was brought to the American continent from the Mediterranean countries and now is avidly cultivated in American gardens and commonly used at the table. Today we can find several varieties of eggplants, of all colors, shapes, and sizes, in American gardens.

From a nutritional point of view, the eggplant possesses few calories, being principally composed of water. But from a medicinal point of view, it possesses diuretic and anticholesterol attributes, which may compensate for its otherwise low nutritional value.

In our monastery kitchen, the eggplant is associated with other products and flavors from Mediterranean countries—where the preparation of eggplant dishes became an art form—such as garlic, onions, olive oil and olive fruits, tomatoes, basil, thyme, rosemary, and other herbs. Occasionally, I like to try some Middle Eastern recipes in which eggplant is the principal element.

STUFFED EGGPLANTS WITH TOMATO SAUCE

4 SERVINGS

4 small to medium eggplants
5 tablespoons olive oil
1 onion, sliced
1 garlic clove, minced
6 sprigs fresh parsley, chopped
1 egg, beaten
salt and pepper to taste
pinch cumin
parsley, freshly chopped, as garnish

Quick Tomato Sauce
5 ripe tomatoes
1 medium onion
2 garlic cloves
a few sprigs parsley, chopped
4 tablespoons olive oil
salt and pepper to taste

1. Slice the eggplants evenly in half lengthwise. Place them in a pan with salted water for about 1 hour. Drain them and scoop out the insides of each half carefully, leaving the shells intact. Chop the eggplant insides; set aside.

2. Preheat the oven to 350°F. Pour the oil into a frying pan. Add the chopped insides of the eggplant and the onion, garlic, and parsley. Sauté gently for 2–3 minutes over medium heat. Remove from the heat and add the beaten egg, salt and pepper, and cumin, and mix well.

3. Fill the eggplant shells with the vegetable-egg mixture. Place the eggplants in a well-buttered baking dish, cover with aluminum foil, and bake for 30 minutes.

4. To prepare the French-style tomato sauce, place the tomatoes, onion, garlic cloves, and parsley in a food processor and blend well. Pour the olive oil into a deep pan, add the tomato mixture, and cook slowly over medium-low heat, stirring often until the mixture reduces and turns into a sauce (about 20 minutes). Add salt and pepper to taste.

5. Remove the eggplants from the oven, place them on warmed plates, and pour the tomato sauce over each. Sprinkle chopped parsley over the top and serve hot.

EGGPLANT AU GRATIN

4 SERVINGS

2 large eggplants, cut into 1-inch-thick round slices
pinch salt
6 large tomatoes
1 large onion
3 garlic cloves
8 basil leaves
a few fresh oregano or thyme leaves
salt and pepper to taste
olive oil as needed
bread crumbs as needed

1. Place the eggplant slices in a large container filled with water. Add salt to the container. Stir a few times and let the eggplant rest for 1 hour. After 1 hour, dry the eggplant slices.

2. In the meantime, slice the tomatoes, onion, and garlic cloves and place them in a food processor or blender. Add the basil, oregano or thyme, and salt and pepper to taste and blend the mixture until it becomes a puree.

3. Preheat the oven to 350°F. Thoroughly oil a baking dish and evenly distribute half the eggplant slices on the bottom. Cover them with half the tomato-herb mixture and repeat the process with a second layer of both. Sprinkle some olive oil on the top of the second layer of the tomato mixture and cover the entire surface with the bread crumbs. Place the dish in the oven for 30 minutes. Remove from the oven and allow to cool for a few minutes before serving.

EGGPLANT SOUTHERN FRENCH STYLE

6 SERVINGS

4 large eggplants
6 tomatoes
5 garlic cloves, minced
1 tablespoon fresh thyme, chopped
6 tablespoons fresh basil, finely chopped
1 tablespoon fresh rosemary, chopped
salt and pepper to taste
1^1/$_2$ cups olive oil

1. Cut the eggplants into thick slices and place them in a pan with salted water for at least 1 hour.

2. Wash and slice the tomatoes. Drain the eggplant slices.

3. Preheat the oven to 350°F. Butter or oil a long ovenproof dish and make a row of eggplant slices alternating with sliced tomatoes in between. Repeat the rows until you have used up the eggplant and tomatoes, inserting the garlic and herbs in between the layers. Sprinkle salt and pepper on top.

4. Before you put the dish in the oven, pour the olive oil equally over the surface of the vegetables. Cover the dish with aluminum foil and place in the oven for 50–60 minutes. Serve hot.

MOTHER STEPHEN'S EGGPLANT ROLLS

4 SERVINGS

2 large, long eggplants
4 tablespoons olive oil
salt and freshly ground pepper to taste
$^1/_2$ cup ricotta cheese
$^1/_2$ cup goat cheese
1 teaspoon dried thyme (or 3 teaspoons fresh)
3 tablespoons fresh basil, minced
1 tablespoon dried rosemary (or 3 tablespoons fresh)
2 cups marinara sauce
$^1/_2$ cup shredded fontina cheese

1. Preheat the oven to 450°F.

2. Cut off eggplant stems. Slice eggplants lengthwise into $^1/_4$ inch-thick slices. Brush the slices on both sides with olive oil and season with salt and pepper. Lay the slices on a well-oiled baking sheet. Cover with foil and roast the eggplant slices for about 10 minutes (turn them over after 5 minutes so they don't stick to the cooking sheet).

3. In a deep bowl combine the ricotta, goat cheese, and herbs. Mix well.

4. Coat a long baking dish thoroughly with cooking oil. Spoon $^3/_4$ cup of the marinara sauce into the bottom of the baking dish. Spread 2 tablespoons of the cheese-herb mixture on each eggplant slice; then roll up the slice and put a toothpick through the center to hold it. Place all the eggplant rolls seam side down in the baking dish. Top them with the remaining marinara sauce and sprinkle the fontina on top.

5. Lower the oven to 350°F. Bake the rolls for 15–20 minutes, until the cheese melts and begins to turn brown. Serve the eggplant rolls warm, 1–2 per plate, as a pleasant appetizer to a good dinner.

EGGPLANT CAVIAR

This eggplant caviar can be used as a dip with crackers or slices of toasted bread. It can also be used as a filling for tomatoes or hard-boiled eggs.

4 large eggplants
6 tablespoons olive oil
4 tomatoes, peeled, seeded, and cut into cubes
2 shallots (or 1 medium onion), minced
1 large garlic clove, minced
$1/4$ cup fresh parsley and fresh thyme, finely chopped, to taste
salt and pepper to taste
1 (8-ounce) container low-fat sour cream

1. Slice the eggplants in 4 quarters lengthwise. Pour 3 tablespoons olive oil into a large frying pan and cook the eggplants for 12 minutes over medium-low heat. Turn them often and add more oil if needed. When the eggplants are cooked thoroughly, set them aside and allow them to cool. Then carefully separate the pulp from the peel. Discard the peel and use a big knife to chop the pulp finely. Set aside.

2. In a deep bowl, place the cubed tomatoes. Add the remaining 3 tablespoons olive oil, the shallots or onion, garlic, parsley and thyme, and salt and pepper. Mix well. Add the chopped eggplant and mix some more. Cover the bowl and place it in the refrigerator for at least 2 hours.

3. Just before serving, take the bowl out of the refrigerator. Adjust the seasonings if necessary, add the sour cream, and mix all the ingredients with a fork until the mixture achieves an even consistency.

Monastery Eggplant Ratatouille

4–6 SERVINGS

4 medium eggplants
pinch salt
2 large onions
$1/3$ cup olive oil
6 tomatoes, peeled, seeded, and chopped
3 zucchini, sliced
2 peppers (one red and one yellow), sliced lengthwise
4 garlic cloves, minced
1 cup (6 ounces) pitted black olives
1 bouquet garni of Provençal herbs (bay leaves, thyme, basil,
    parsley, and rosemary tied together with a thin thread)
salt and pepper to taste

1. Slice the eggplants and place them in a container with fresh water and salt for 1 hour. Rinse in cold water and drain them thoroughly.

2. Slice the onions and sauté them in the olive oil in a Dutch oven or cast-iron saucepan over medium-low heat for 2–3 minutes.

3. Add the tomatoes and the eggplant, stir well, and cover the saucepan. Cook for 4–5 minutes over medium-high heat.

4. Add the zucchini, peppers, garlic, olives, bouquet garni, and salt and pepper. Stir well and cover the saucepan again. Reduce the heat to low and cook for 25–30 minutes, until most of the liquid evaporates. Stir from time to time to avoid burning the bottom.

5. When the ratatouille is done, discard the bouquet garni and serve hot or refrigerate it for several hours and serve cold.

ENDIVES

(Cichorium endivia)

The present-day endive was originally a wild chicory (*C. intybus*) until one day, around 1850, a certain Mr. Bressiers, in charge of the botanical gardens in Brussels, Belgium, discovered the process of transforming ordinary chicory into what he called *chicon de chicorée* in French, *witloof* in Flemish (which means "white leaves"). Mr. Bressiers achieved success in this enterprise by cultivating the chicories in his basement, where there was no contact with the light.

Today, endives are primarily cultivated in Belgium and northern France, which supply the world market. That is why they tend to be a bit expensive at the supermarket.

Nutritionally, the endive contains potassium and other vitamins and is especially low in calories. That is one of the reasons it is popular among Europeans who are concerned about controlling their weight. At the American table, the endive is usually preferred fresh in salads, but it can be used equally well in cooked dishes, as some of the recipes here demonstrate. Its fine delicate flavor adds grace and distinction to any dish in which it is used.

ENDIVE AND BEER SOUP GRATINÉE

This soup is a delicious introduction to an elegant winter dinner.

6 SERVINGS

8 medium Belgian endives
6 tablespoons butter or margarine
6 (12-ounce) bottles beer (ale or pilsner)
3 vegetable bouillon cubes
salt, freshly ground pepper, and nutmeg to taste
6 slices bread
grated Gruyère cheese (or other cheese of your preference)

1. Wash the endives well and cut them in half lengthwise. Slice them very fine and then mince them. Melt the butter in a good-size deep saucepan, add the endives, and sauté lightly over low heat for a few minutes. Add the beer, bouillon cubes, and seasonings. Stir well and cook over medium-low heat for 20–25 minutes.

2. While the soup is cooking, melt a bit of butter in a frying pan and lightly brown both sides of the bread slices. Set aside.

3. Preheat the oven to 300°F. When the soup is done, pour it evenly into six ovenproof bowls. Place 1 slice of bread on the top of each bowl and cover it with grated Gruyère cheese. Put the bowls in the oven for 15–20 minutes and serve when the cheese is melted and the soup is boiling hot. In other words, when the soup is well gratinéed.

ENDIVES FLEMISH STYLE

This dish can be served as an appetizer or as an accompaniment to the main course.

4 SERVINGS

4 large endives
2 tablespoons butter
2 shallots, minced
2 tablespoons honey
1 lemon rind
8 ounces beer
3 tablespoons heavy cream
$^1/4$ cup fresh parsley, finely chopped, as garnish
salt and pepper to taste
2 hard-boiled eggs, chopped and crumbled, as garnish
parsley, finely chopped, as garnish

1. Clean and trim the endives at their base, discarding their bitter part. With a thin knife, slice them carefully in half lengthwise.

2. Melt the butter in a large, heavy skillet. Add the shallots, honey, and lemon rind and cook over medium-low heat for 2 minutes. Stir frequently so that the shallots don't overcook.

3. Place the endive halves, interior sides down, over the shallots and cook for about 1 minute. Add the beer, heavy cream, chopped parsley, and salt and pepper and cover the skillet. Continue cooking over low heat for about 15 minutes.

4. When the endives are done, place two halves on each serving plate with the inner part facing up. Pour some of the creamy sauce from the pan on top of each and sprinkle crumbled hard-boiled eggs and chopped parsley on top. Serve immediately.

ENDIVE SOUP DUTCH STYLE

This soup can be served at the start of a special or elegant dinner.

6 SERVINGS

5 large Belgian endives
2 ounces butter or margarine
2 medium onions, minced
6 cups water
2 potatoes, peeled and diced
1 bouillon cube (flavor of your choice)
salt to taste
nutmeg to taste
1 egg
4 tablespoons heavy cream
fresh parsley, finely chopped, as garnish

1. Wash and clean the endives well. Slice them into half-inch pieces.

2. Melt the butter in a soup pot and add the endives and onions. Sauté lightly over medium-low heat for approximately 2 minutes then add 4 cups of the water. Bring to a boil. Cover the pot and cook for 10 minutes.

3. In a separate pot, place the potatoes and the remaining 2 cups of water. Bring to a boil and cook the potatoes for 1 minute until they are tender. Once they are cooked, remove the pot from the heat and whirl its contents in a blender or food processor.

4. Pour the potatoes into the pot with the endives. Add the bouillon cube, salt, and nutmeg and continue cooking over medium-low heat for another 5 minutes to bring to a boil. Remove from heat.

5. Just before serving, beat an egg in a small bowl, add the cream, and beat some more until it is well blended. Pour this mixture into the soup and blend it thoroughly. Serve the soup hot and garnish with chopped parsley.

HUDSON VALLEY SHALLOT DIP

This dip can be served on crackers, thinly sliced French bread, endive leaves, or other crudités.

6–8 SERVINGS

5 teaspoons olive oil
12 shallots, thinly sliced
2 teaspoons cider vinegar
1 cup Chatham Blue cheese (from sheep's milk), crumbled
1 (8-ounce) container low-fat sour cream
5 tablespoons finely chopped fresh chives
endive leaves (optional)

1. Pour the oil into a skillet. Add the shallots and sauté over low-medium heat about 2 minutes, until golden. Add the vinegar and mix well. Sauté for about 10 minutes, stirring frequently. Remove from heat and allow to cool.

2. Combine the cheese and sour cream in a blender and process until smooth. Pour the mixture into a serving bowl. Add the shallots and chives and mix well. Adjust the seasonings as desired and add salt and pepper to taste. Refrigerate for several hours before serving.

FENNEL

(Foeniculum dulce)

Fennel is a vegetable of Mediterranean origin. The ancient Egyptians, the Greeks, and the Romans all used it often for medicinal and therapeutic purposes. In the Middle Ages, however, especially during times of famine, the Italians began serving fennel more frequently, and in a variety of ways. At the turn of the last century, fennel was also introduced into Provence, the region of France nearest to Italy, where it has become a staple of the Provençal table.

Though popular in Italy and southern France, fennel has not fared as well in northern Europe or other countries with colder climates, and it remains to this day a regional Mediterranean product. It was, of course, the Italians who introduced fennel to the United States, where it recently has become quite popular in certain kitchens.

Fennel is a fascinating and quite intriguing vegetable with a subtle flavor all its own. When eaten raw in a salad, its has a light licorice flavor, and the freshness of its texture is a treat to the palate. When cooked, however, fennel changes its character, developing a milder and sweeter taste. When cooking fennel, it is always helpful to add a bit of lemon juice and salt to the boiling water, which protects and enhances its taste. When selecting fennel at the market, it is important to check the freshness of the bulb. Smaller bulbs are usually best, for they cook more quickly and can also be presented whole at the table.

Fennel can be eaten and served in a variety of ways. Because of its licorice-like taste, it is a good accompaniment to any dish in which fish plays the central role. It also blends well with tomatoes, onions, and zucchini when cooked, or in a salad with endives, tomatoes, and other compatible vegetables uncooked. When eaten raw, a dash of lemon juice or balsamic vinegar accentuates its subtle flavor.

Fennel Ratatouille

This dish is a good accompaniment to fish served cold during the summer months.

6 fennel bulbs
4 large tomatoes
6 tablespoons olive oil, plus more if needed
salt and freshly ground pepper to taste
a few leaves of fresh basil, finely chopped

1. Wash and clean the fennel bulbs well. Trim the stalks and root ends and cut away any bruised parts. Cut the fennel in even slices.

2. Boil the tomatoes for about 10 minutes, then peel them and remove their seeds. Chop the remainder finely.

3. Pour the oil into a deep skillet, add the fennel, and sauté lightly over low heat for about 5 minutes, until it is cooked. Add the tomatoes and salt and pepper and continue cooking for another 5 minutes, stirring frequently. (Add more oil if needed.)

4. When the vegetables are cooked, place them in a deep bowl or dish, add the finely chopped basil, and allow the vegetables to cool. Refrigerate the ratatouille for at least an hour then serve cold as an elegant appetizer.

Braised Fennel

This dish is an excellent appetizer. It also accompanies a fish main course well.

6 SERVINGS

4 fennel bulbs
5 tablespoons olive oil
1 onion, sliced
3 tomatoes, peeled, seeded, and finely chopped
8 basil leaves, finely chopped
salt and pepper to taste
2 tablespoons balsamic vinegar
$^1/_2$ cup pitted black olives (optional)

1. Trim the fennel and slice each bulb into quarters. Pour the olive oil into a large, fairly deep skillet. Add the sliced onion and sauté gently over medium-low heat for several minutes.

2. Add the fennel and continue cooking with the saucepan covered for at least 5 minutes. Add the chopped tomatoes, basil, salt and pepper, vinegar, and black olives. Stir a few times, re-cover the saucepan, and continue cooking for 2–3 more minutes. Toss the vegetables gently and be careful that they do not burn or stick at the bottom. Serve hot or at least warm.

Saint Gregory's Fennel Casserole

Saint Gregory, called "the Great," was the first pope who previously was a monk. Even after being elected pope, he continued living as a monk in his own monastery of Saint Andrew. He was not only a very holy man, but also a very talented writer. Among the many admirable writings he left behind is the Dialogues, which contains the life of Saint Benedict. His feast is celebrated on September 3.

6–8 SERVINGS

2 medium fennel bulbs
pinch salt
6 tablespoons olive or other oil
1 large onion, sliced
6 large tomatoes, peeled, seeded, and chopped
4 garlic cloves, minced
2 zucchini, sliced
2 yellow squash, sliced
16 fresh basil leaves, finely chopped
salt and pepper to taste
½ cup grated Cheddar or other cheese

1. Remove the stalks and the outer layers of the fennel bulbs. Slice them into about 2-inch squares. Place them in a saucepan with cold water to cover, add salt, and let stand for an hour. Drain and set aside.

2. Pour the oil into a large, heavy saucepan and add the onion, tomatoes, and garlic. Cook over medium-low heat for about 4–5 minutes. Stir frequently.

3. Add the fennel, zucchini, squash, basil, and salt and pepper to the saucepan and mix well. Cover and reduce the heat to low, and continue cooking for another 5 minutes. Stir from time to time.

4. Preheat the oven to 300°F. Thoroughly butter an ovenproof casserole dish and spoon the vegetables with their sauce into it. Cover the top with grated cheese and bake for 25–30 minutes, until the cheese has melted. Serve hot.

GRAINS & CEREALS

Among the grains and cereals, rice and wheat probably know a longer history than most others. The ancient world was already aware of them as much as 5,000 years ago. Their point of origin, however, remains a mystery that is debated by botanists of our time.

Rice, in particular, has gained universal acceptance and throughout the centuries has become the main staple in a number of cultures. For example, rice is the fundamental element in the diet of people in China, Japan, Indonesia, India, and the various countries of Southeast Asia. In China, there is an ancient saying that states, "A meal without rice is like a beautiful woman with only one eye." This saying portrays vividly the place and value attributed to rice in Chinese culture. Many other cultures with long histories attest to the same truth.

The existence of rice was discovered by Westerners through Alexander the Great during one of his trips in the Mesopotamia region of Asia. His soldiers carried samples of rice back to the Mediterranean Basin, where it was incorporated into Greek and Roman cultures. In later centuries, the Moors introduced rice to the Spanish kitchen, and during the Middle Ages, the returning Crusaders were responsible for the appearance of rice in French and Italian cooking. The French in particular took to incorporating rice into various dishes, as its foreign origin added an exotic touch to the table. In spite of the curiosity surrounding this grain, however, one has to wait until well into the fourteenth and fifteenth centuries to see the cultivation of rice extended throughout Western continental Europe, where it has now become an accepted staple.

Today rice is a basic, universal grain that nourishes more than half of the world's people. There are over 8,000 varieties of rice cultivated throughout the world. The Asian countries, as one expects, are the main suppliers of rice to the world market.

Wheat is one of the earliest grains to be domesticated by man. Used as flour, it is the chief grain in the West. Different types of wheat find different applications: The harder wheats are used to make pasta, while softer varieties go to make bread. Wheat grain is also used as bulgur (parched cracked wheat) and other forms.

Grains in general are part and parcel of a healthy diet. With the newfound health consciousness among people today, grains have regained their rightful place in the daily fare of those who strive to establish a healthy balance in their eating habits. While rice and wheat remain the better-known and most widely consumed cereal grains, others such as millet, alfalfa, and barley are increasingly incorporated into the grain menu by those who seek to achieve a nutritious diet.

Saffron Rice Provençal Style

4–6 SERVINGS

8 tablespoons olive oil
1 medium onion, chopped
1 red pepper, diced
2 garlic cloves, minced
8 black olives, chopped
2$\frac{1}{2}$ cups uncooked basmati rice
large pinch of saffron threads
salt and white pepper to taste
4 cups water
2 cups dry white wine

1. Pour the oil into a Dutch oven; add the onion and pepper. Sauté lightly for about 2 minutes over medium-low heat.

2. Add the garlic, olives, and rice and continue cooking over medium-low heat for 3–4 minutes. Stir frequently. Add the saffron and salt and pepper and stir some more.

3. Mix the water and the wine in a separate saucepan and bring to a boil. Add the water-wine mixture gradually to the rice. Stir continuously until all the liquid is absorbed. Serve hot.

(Another way of cooking the rice is to pour the water-wine mixture over the rice and mix it well, then cover the Dutch oven and place it in a 350°F preheated oven for 25–30 minutes, or until all the liquid is absorbed. Take the pot out, uncover it, and let stand for 5 minutes before serving.)

RISOTTO DELLA CERTOSINA

Serve freshly grated Parmesan cheese on the side for those who wish to add more to their plates.

6–8 SERVINGS

$1/2$ cup good-quality olive oil
1 cup sliced porcini mushrooms
1 large onion, chopped
3 garlic cloves, minced
1 cup cooked white beans or 1 (8-ounce) can, rinsed
    and drained
1 cup pitted small black olives (6-ounce jar, drained)
4 tomatoes, peeled, seeded, and chopped
3 tablespoons butter
2 cups uncooked Arborio rice
4 cups water or vegetable stock
1 bottle (750 mL) dry white wine
1 bay leaf
1 celery stalk, thinly sliced
2 tablespoons lemon juice
a few parsley sprigs, finely chopped
salt and pepper to taste
$1/3$ cup grated Parmesan cheese

1. Pour the olive oil into a large Dutch oven or cast-iron casserole. Place the mushrooms and the onion in the pan and sauté lightly for about 3 minutes over medium-low heat. Stir frequently.

2. After 3 minutes, add the garlic, white beans (these may also be added later, after the rice), olives, and tomatoes, and continue cooking over medium-low heat for another 3 minutes. Stir frequently.

3. Add the butter and the rice and stir continuously. While the vegetables are being sautéed, mix the water (or stock) and wine in a separate saucepan and bring to a quick boil. Keep it simmering afterward.

4. Add the bay leaf, celery, lemon juice, parsley, and salt and pepper to the rice and mix well. Add 2 cups of the water-wine mixture immediately after and stir continuously. When most of the liquid has been absorbed, add another 2 cups and repeat the process until the rice is cooked.

5. When the rice is done and all the liquid has evaporated, discard the bay leaf and add the Parmesan cheese, gently mixing it with the risotto. Serve the risotto on hot plates.

TRANSFIGURATION RICE PILAF

The beautiful feast of the Transfiguration of the Lord is celebrated on August 6. It is dearly loved by all monks and nuns, for the light of Tabor, which shone from Jesus' face, sanctifies all those who come close to him. The feast of the Transfiguration is also the feast of the harvest, and in the monastery we keep the custom of bringing in offering to the church the vegetables, fruits, and flowers of our gardens. After the Liturgy, the traditional blessing is bestowed upon our produce, symbolizing that the earth itself is made new by the presence of the transfigured Christ.

4–6 SERVINGS

6 tablespoons olive oil
1 large onion, coarsely chopped
12 mushrooms, finely chopped
2 cups uncooked rice
2^1/2 cups water
2^1/2 cups dry white wine
1 bouillon cube (flavor of your choice)
1 teaspoon dried thyme (or 3 teaspoons fresh)
1 bay leaf
salt and pepper to taste

1. Pour the olive oil into a cast-iron saucepan and sauté the onion and the mushrooms over medium-low heat for 2–3 minutes. Add the rice and stir constantly.

2. Mix the water and the wine in a separate saucepan and bring to a boil. Then pour the mixture into the rice, add the bouillon cube, thyme, bay leaf, and salt and pepper and stir.

3. Cover the pot and cook slowly over medium-low heat. Stir the rice from time to time so it does not burn on the bottom. When all the liquid has been absorbed, remove the bay leaf and serve the rice while it is hot.

Saint Paschal's Barley Soup

Paschal Baylon was a seventeenth-century saint from Spain. As a young man, he was a sheepherder prior to joining the community of the order of Friars Minor at Loreto. He was known to have an extraordinary devotion to the Blessed Sacrament, and his humble demeanor was a source of inspiration to his community. His feast day is May 17.

4–6 SERVINGS

6 tablespoons olive oil
2 onions, chopped
3 carrots, diced
1 celery heart, chopped
1 cup sliced mushrooms
4 garlic cloves, minced
8 cups water
1 cup uncooked barley
1 cup white wine
1 vegetable bouillon cube
salt and pepper
1/3 cup fresh parsley, chopped
4–6 teaspoons sour cream

1. Pour the oil in a heated saucepan and gently sauté the onions, carrots, celery, mushrooms, and garlic over low heat for about 3 minutes. Stir often.

2. Add the water, barley, wine, bouillon cube, and salt and pepper and bring to a boil. Lower the heat, cover the pot, and simmer slowly for 45–50 minutes. Add the parsley, stir well, and turn off the heat. Cover the pot and let the soup rest for 10 minutes.

3. Serve the soup and place 1 teaspoon sour cream at the center of each serving.

Risotto Primavera

Parmesan or other similar grated cheese can be added to the risotto just before it finishes cooking.

6–8 SERVINGS

1 zucchini
^{1}/3 cup olive oil
1 large red onion, chopped
2 cups uncooked Arborio rice
3 cups water or vegetable stock
3 cups dry white wine
16 asparagus stalks, cut into 1-inch slices
1 cup snow peas, shelled or frozen
1 cup fava beans
4 tablespoons fresh parsley, chopped
1 teaspoon dried thyme
salt and white pepper to taste

1. Cut the zucchini in quarters lengthwise and then into 1-inch-thick slices; set aside.

2. Pour the oil into a good-size cast-iron saucepan or Dutch oven. Add the onion and sauté lightly over medium-low heat for 3–4 minutes. Add the rice and continue cooking for another 3 minutes, stirring constantly.

3. While stirring the onion and rice, mix the water and wine in a separate saucepan and bring to a boil; keep the mixture simmering.

4. Gradually add 2 cups of the water-wine mixture to the rice while stirring continuously. When the liquid has been absorbed, add the zucchini, asparagus, peas, fava beans, parsley, thyme, and salt and pepper.

5. Immediately add 2 more cups of the water-wine mixture and continue cooking, stirring continuously. When most of the liquid has been absorbed, check the seasonings and continue to gradually add the remaining water-wine mixture until all the liquid has been absorbed and the rice is creamy and tender. Cover the pot and serve immediately while the rice is hot.

TABOULI SALAD

This is an excellent salad to serve during the hot summer months or early in the fall season.

6 SERVINGS

1 cup uncooked bulgur
1 pound cherry tomatoes, trimmed and sliced in half
1 medium Vidalia onion, chopped
1 medium cucumber, peeled, seeded, and cut into cubes
1/2 cup fresh parsley, finely chopped
1/4 cup fresh mint, finely chopped
1/3 cup olive oil
5 tablespoons freshly squeezed lemon juice
salt and freshly ground pepper to taste

1. The night before the salad is to be prepared, place the bulgur in a medium casserole and fill it with cold water to about half its size. Let the bulgur stand for several hours, until you are ready to use it. Just before preparing the salad, drain the bulgur into a strainer, rinse it in cold water, and again drain it thoroughly so that no excess water remains.

2. Place all the vegetables in a deep salad bowl.

3. Prepare the tabouli by mixing in a separate bowl the well-drained bulgur, parsley, mint, oil, lemon juice, and salt and pepper. Mix well.

4. Add the bulgur mixture to the vegetables in the salad bowl. Toss and mix well. The salad can be refrigerated for 1 hour before serving.

JERUSALEM ARTICHOKES

(Helianthus tuberosus)

Around 1603, a certain man named Champlain, a governor of Canada at that time, discovered a root vegetable that was quite popular among the Huron Indians of the region. This vegetable, today the Jerusalem artichoke, or *topinambour* in French, was believed to be part of the daily diet of the Indians. From Canada it spread to France and other places on the European continent. The French, in particular, became very interested in this root vegetable because they found that its taste was similar to that of the artichoke. This is why it was known in France by the name *artichaut du Canada*, which in due time led to the English name of Jerusalem artichoke for this vegetable. The name Jerusalem came not from the city of Jerusalem but from the Italian girasole, or "sunflower." This was appropriate since the flower of the Jerusalem artichoke resembled a miniature sunflower. Both the Jerusalem artichoke and the sunflower belong to the family Helianthus, which means "flower of the sun."

The plant of the Jerusalem artichoke is a perennial, and one must be extra careful about the place of its cultivation because it spreads easily and can overtake the rest of the garden. Such is the case in our own garden, where every year we face the task of trying to contain and confine its cultivation to a small section of the garden.

The Jerusalem artichoke became popular again in France during the war years, where it was often substituted for the potato. One of its advantages is that its cultivation is easy. It continues to grow and prosper even in times of drought and in the poorest soils.

JERUSALEM ARTICHOKES BASQUE STYLE

Serve this as an accompaniment to egg, fish, and meat dishes.

12 artichokes, cleaned and diced
4 tablespoons olive oil
1 onion, chopped
3 garlic cloves, minced
6 tablespoons fresh parsley, minced
salt to taste
pinch nutmeg

1. Place the diced artichokes in boiling water to cover and cook over medium heat for about 5 minutes. Drain and set aside.

2. Pour some olive oil into a nonstick skillet and add the onion and garlic. Cook over medium-low heat 2–3 minutes, until the onion begins to turn. Stir frequently.

3. Add the artichokes, parsley, salt, and nutmeg. Stir and continue cooking for 2 more minutes. Serve hot.

JERUSALEM ARTICHOKE SOUP

4–6 SERVINGS

1 pound Jerusalem artichokes
4 tablespoons olive oil
2 medium onions, chopped (or 3 leeks, white parts only, chopped)
4 tablespoons lemon juice
7 cups vegetable broth or water
salt and pepper to taste
pinch nutmeg
1 (8-ounce) container half-and-half
1 bunch tarragon leaves, finely chopped, as garnish

1. Wash the Jerusalem artichokes well and dice.

2. Pour the oil into a large saucepan and add the onions. Sauté lightly over low heat for 3–4 minutes. Add the diced Jerusalem artichokes and sprinkle the lemon juice over them. Stir and mix well. Cook over medium-low heat for about 5 minutes, stirring often.

3. Add the broth or water, salt and pepper, and nutmeg and bring to a boil. Continue cooking for another 15–20 minutes over medium-low heat, until the vegetables are well cooked. Whirl the soup in a food processor and then return it to the saucepan. Add the half-and-half. Reheat over medium-low heat, stirring continuously, for 2–3 minutes. Serve the soup hot and sprinkle some chopped tarragon on the top of each serving as a garnish.

JERUSALEM ARTICHOKES FROM THE ARDÈCHES

This is good as an accompaniment to egg, fish, and meat dishes.

4–6 SERVINGS

1 pound Jerusalem artichokes
8 tablespoons saffron or other oil
3 garlic cloves, chopped, plus 1 garlic clove, minced
1 (8-ounce) container sour cream or plain yogurt
2 tablespoons fresh tarragon, finely chopped
    (or 1 teaspoon dried)
salt and pepper to taste

1. Wash the artichokes well. Peel and cut them into large chunks.

2. Pour the oil into a large, deep skillet and heat it over medium-low heat. Add the artichoke chunks and the three chopped garlic cloves. Cook for 12–15 minutes, stirring frequently so the mixture does not stick or burn on the bottom.

3. Place the sour cream in a deep bowl. Add the tarragon and the remaining garlic clove (minced) and mix well with a fork. After the artichokes have cooked, add this creamy mixture to them and sprinkle with salt and pepper. Mix well, stirring several times. Cover the skillet for about 2 minutes, allowing the artichokes to be enveloped by the creamy sauce. Serve hot.

LEEKS

(Allium ampeloprasum)

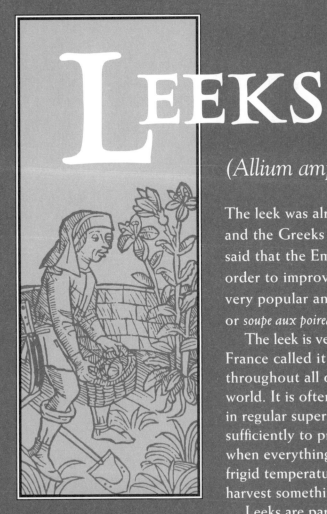

The leek was already known and well used in ancient times. The Egyptians and the Greeks in particular had great appreciation for it. In Rome, it is said that the Emperor Nero consumed a certain amount of leeks daily in order to improve his vocal cords. During the Middle Ages, leeks were very popular and commonly used in the soup appropriately called porée, or *soupe aux poireaux* in French.

The leek is very popular not only in France, where the writer Anatole France called it *l'asperge du pauvre*, or poor man's asparagus, but also throughout all of Europe. And it is now having success in other parts of the world. It is often cultivated in American gardens and can usually be found in regular supermarkets. Here in our monastery garden, we grow leek plants sufficiently to provide for the winter months. In the middle of December, when everything else is dead in the garden, the only things that survive the frigid temperatures are the tall leek plants, and it is a great joy to be able to harvest something from our garden at that time of the year.

Leeks are particularly rich in water and low in calories; they are therefore an easy vegetable to digest and enjoy at the table.

LEEKS FLEMISH STYLE

*This dish makes a wonderful introduction to
a good dinner.*

4 SERVINGS

8 leeks
2 cups milk
3 tablespoons flour
3–4 ounces goat cheese, crumbled
salt and pepper to taste
fresh chervil or parsley, finely chopped, as garnish

1. Wash the leeks well and trim. Cook in salted boiling water to cover for 12 minutes; drain.

2. In a saucepan, mix the milk and flour well. Cook over low heat for about 10 minutes, stirring continuously. Add the goat cheese, leeks, and salt and pepper. Cover the pan and continue cooking over low heat for another 6–7 minutes. Turn off the heat and serve immediately with chopped chervil or parsley on top of each serving.

LEEKS ELIANE ANGER STYLE

4 SERVINGS

8 large leeks
salt

Dressing
8 tablespoons olive oil
4 tablespoons tarragon-scented vinegar
2 ounces goat cheese, crumbled thoroughly with a fork
salt and freshly ground pepper to taste

1. Trim the leeks by cutting off the roots and the green tops. Remove the outer layer. Place the leeks in the top half of a double boiler, add salt, cover, and cook over medium heat for 20 minutes. When the leeks are cooked, drain and run cold water over them. Drain again and set aside.

2. Prepare the dressing by mixing all the ingredients in a small bowl until a consistently smooth sauce is achieved.

3. When ready to serve, place two leeks on each serving plate and pour some of the dressing over each serving. Serve this dish cold as an appetizer.

LEEKS VINAIGRETTE

This is a wonderful appetizer for an elegant dinner.

8 large leeks
3 tomatoes, sliced
1 cucumber, sliced
fresh parsley, finely chopped, as garnish

Vinaigrette
8 tablespoons olive oil
4 tablespoons balsamic vinegar (or any vinegar of choice)
1 teaspoon mustard
salt and freshly ground pepper to taste

1. Trim and clean the leeks well. Separate the white and green parts of the leeks. Slice the white parts in half carefully. (Discard the green parts or use them later in a soup preparation.)

2. Carefully tie the sliced leeks together with string so they remain intact while cooking. Place them with care into boiling salted water. Cover the pot and cook over medium-low heat for 30 minutes. Drain and allow them to cool.

3. When it is time to serve, untie the leeks and place 4 halved leeks on each plate. Surround them on one side with the sliced tomatoes and on the other with the sliced cucumber. Mix all the vinaigrette ingredients together well in a small bowl. Pour the vinaigrette evenly over the vegetables. Sprinkle the chopped parsley on top and serve immediately.

LEEKS GREEK STYLE

This dish makes an attractive appetizer for a good dinner.

4 SERVINGS

8 leeks
1 cup dry white wine
1 cup water
1 bouillon cube (flavor of your choice)
12 small onions (cippolina, shallots, or similar), peeled and trimmed (3 per person)
1 bay leaf
$^1/_2$ cup olive oil
salt to taste
a few whole peppercorns

1. Wash the leeks well. Separate the white parts from the green; discard the green parts. Place the white parts in salted boiling water and blanch for about 4 minutes maximum. Drain carefully.

2. Place the blanched leeks in a saucepan and add the wine, water, bouillon cube, onions, bay leaf, oil, salt, and peppercorns. Cover the pan and cook the leeks and onions over medium-low heat for about 30 minutes, until most of the liquid evaporates. When the vegetables are done, allow them to cool for at least 1 hour before serving. Discard the bay leaf and peppercorns. Place 2 leeks and 3 small onions on each plate and serve.

LEEKS BATONNETS

Serve hot as an appetizer or as an accompaniment to a main course.

8 leeks, trimmed and cut 7 inches long
6 tablespoons flour (approximately)
1 egg, beaten
salt and pepper to taste
bread crumbs
1/3 cup oil (for frying)

1. Place the leeks in salted boiling water, and cook 8–10 minutes. Drain and dry with a paper towel.

2. Place the flour in a flat dish. Beat the egg, add salt and pepper, and beat some more. Place the bread crumbs in another flat dish.

3. Roll each leek cane (batonnet) first in the flour, then in the egg, and then in the bread crumbs.

4. Pour the oil into a skillet over medium-high heat. When it gets very hot, place the leeks in it and cook carefully, seeing that they remain intact and are fried on all sides.

5. Preheat the oven to 300°F. Butter a baking dish thoroughly. Place the fried leeks in the baking dish and bake for 15–20 minutes.

LEEK RISOTTO

4–6 SERVINGS

4 tablespoons butter
1 shallot, minced
2 leeks, washed and thinly sliced (white parts only)
2 cups uncooked Arborio rice
5 cups boiling water (or chicken broth)
1 cup dry white wine
salt and freshly ground black pepper to taste
$1/3$ teaspoon nutmeg
$1/2$ cup grated cheese (Parmesan or other as you prefer),
   plus additional grated cheese for the table

1. Melt the butter in a large, heavy saucepan. Add the shallot and the leeks. Sauté lightly over medium-low heat until they wilt.

2. Add the rice and stir constantly for 1–2 minutes, until it becomes well coated with the sauce and begins to slightly change color. Add the boiling water or broth gradually, stirring constantly, then add the white wine. Add the salt and pepper and nutmeg when half the liquid is absorbed and continue stirring.

3. When the rice is cooked, add the grated cheese and stir vigorously until it is all incorporated into the rice. Serve hot and place additional grated cheese at the table.

MUSHROOMS

(Agaricus)

The mushroom, though not a traditional vegetable cultivated in the garden, has become important in daily culinary use and cannot be ignored in this collection of recipes.

The mushroom, in its many varieties, has a long history. Its cultivation predates that of many vegetables. Mushrooms have been appreciated for thousands of years and have been collected and used in the kitchen by chefs of all backgrounds and cultures. The appeal of the mushroom, or *champignon* in French, is universal. Some claim that it has healing qualities that make it desirable from a medicinal point of view.

Today there is a wide variety of mushrooms. Some are edible, and others are toxic. One must be careful and knowledgeable when collecting wild mushrooms for the table—prudence and discretion in this area are the order of the day. Among the well-known mushroom varieties or "fungi," as mushrooms are sometimes called, are the white supermarket mushroom (*Agaricus bisporus*)—which is probably domestically the most popular—the chanterelle, the porcini, the portobello, the cèpe, the shiitake, and, of course, the morel and the truffle, which are among the most cherished by good cooks and a true delight to the palate.

Though mushrooms are not cultivated at the monastery, they are frequently used in the monastery kitchen. I have fond memories of walking in the woods with my grandmother and picking varieties of wild mushrooms, especially during the spring and autumn months. Today when I go back to France, it warms my heart to see that this ancient practice continues to this day. It is common to see people off the country roads or in the woods with their paniers, picking the choicest gifts Mother Nature gives us.

MUSHROOMS AU GRATIN

This dish can be served as a main course for a light lunch or brunch.

4 SERVINGS

6 tablespoons butter
20 large mushrooms, cleaned and sliced
3 carrots, peeled and sliced into small cubes
4 shallots, minced
$^1/_3$ cup fresh parsley, chopped
2 cups dry white wine
salt and pepper to taste
grated cheese of your preference

1. Melt the butter in a deep saucepan. Add the mushrooms, carrots, shallots, and parsley. Stir well, cover the saucepan, and cook over low heat for about 10 minutes. Add the wine, stir thoroughly, and continue cooking until the wine reduces by half. Add the seasonings and again stir thoroughly.

2. Preheat the oven to 250°F. Butter a round ovenproof dish, sprinkle some grated cheese over the butter, and distribute the mushroom mixture with its remaining liquid evenly over the dish. Cover the top with more grated cheese and place the dish in the oven until the cheese is evenly melted. Serve immediately.

Greek-Style Mushroom Salad

This salad should always be served cold and mainly as an appetizer.

$^1/_2$ pound mushrooms
juice of 1 lemon
1 (8-ounce) can artichoke hearts, drained
2 garlic cloves, minced
4 small zucchini (the fresher and newer, the better)
$^1/_2$ pound feta cheese, cut into small chunks

Vinaigrette
6 tablespoons olive oil
juice of 1 lemon
1 teaspoon fresh thyme (or $^1/_3$ teaspoon dried)
1 teaspoon fresh rosemary (or $^1/_3$ teaspoon dried)
salt and pepper to taste

1. Clean the mushrooms well. Slice them and place them in a bowl. Add the lemon juice, toss the mushrooms, and set aside.

2. Rinse the canned artichokes in cold water and drain thoroughly. Add them to the mushrooms along with the garlic. Wash the zucchini and cut them into thin slices. Add to the bowl.

3. Add the feta cheese to the vegetables in the bowl and toss once more. Place the bowl in the refrigerator until you are ready to serve.

4. Just before serving, prepare the vinaigrette by mixing the olive oil, lemon juice, thyme, rosemary, and salt and pepper in a small bowl. Pour this vinaigrette over the vegetables and cheese. Toss everything well until equally mixed.

MUSHROOM MEDLEY

This makes a nice appetizer.

6–8 SERVINGS

$^1/_2$ pound mushrooms
1 (8-ounce) jar artichokes
1 (10-ounce) jar cocktail onions
4 small zucchini
2 (1$^1/_2$-ounce) packages white raisins
3 cups dry white wine
1 cup water
6 tablespoons tomato paste
$^1/_4$ cup olive oil, plus extra as garnish
1 bay leaf
pinch thyme (fresh or dried)
a few parsley sprigs, finely chopped
salt and pepper to taste

1. Clean the mushrooms well. Chop coarsely and set aside. Drain the artichokes and the onions thoroughly and set aside. Slice the zucchini into small thin pieces.

2. Place the mushrooms, artichokes, onions, and zucchini in a good-size saucepan. Add the raisins, wine, water, tomato paste, $^1/_4$ cup olive oil, bay leaf, thyme, parsley, and salt and pepper. Cook the medley over medium-low heat for about 20 minutes. Allow it to cool.

3. Place the medley in a deep glass bowl, cover, and refrigerate for 24 hours. When ready to serve, remove the bay leaf and drain the juice from the vegetables. Serve the medley cold, in individual dishes, and pour a bit of olive oil over each serving.

Saint Odile Mushroom Velouté

This is a delicious velouté to be served as an appetizer for a good dinner.

4–6 SERVINGS

2 ounces dried mushrooms (porcini or other)
1 cup water
5 garlic cloves
1 pound fresh mushrooms
3 tablespoons olive oil
6 cups vegetable (or chicken) broth
salt and pepper to taste
$^{1}/_{2}$ pint heavy cream
fresh parsley, finely chopped

1. Place the dried mushrooms in a saucepan. Add the water and bring the mushrooms to a boil for 3–4 minutes. Turn off the heat and let them rest for 10 minutes.

2. Peel and mince the garlic cloves. Clean the fresh mushrooms thoroughly. Slice thin and combine with the garlic.

3. Pour the oil into a good-size soup pot and heat over low-medium heat. Immediately add the garlic-mushroom mixture and the broth. Add the salt and pepper. Cook the mixture for 7–8 minutes over medium heat.

4. Pour the cream into a blender. Add the cooked dried mushrooms together with their liquid and the chopped parsley. Blend the mixture thoroughly and then pour it into the soup pot. Continue cooking for 3 more minutes and then serve very hot.

MUSTARDY MUSHROOM SAUCE

This sauce can be served over certain meat dishes or noodles. It can also be used as a dip and goes well with slices of toasted bread.

6–8 SERVINGS

1 pound porcini mushrooms
2 tablespoons spicy Dijon mustard
1 (8-ounce) container low-fat sour cream
2 garlic cloves
1 lemon
2 ounces butter
salt and freshly ground pepper to taste

1. Clean the mushrooms well. Chop them into small pieces.

2. Place the mustard and the sour cream in a deep bowl. Mix thoroughly, using a fork.

3. Peel and finely chop the garlic; set aside. Extract all the juice from the lemon into a small bowl; set aside.

4. Melt the butter in a deep frying pan. Add the mushrooms, garlic, lemon juice, and salt and pepper to taste. Cook the mixture for 4–5 minutes over medium-low heat, stirring frequently.

5. Add the mustard–sour cream mixture, raise the heat to medium, and continue cooking for 5 minutes or so, until the mixture achieves an even, creamy consistency. Adjust the seasonings as desired and serve hot.

CHANTERELLE MUSHROOM SALAD

6 SERVINGS

1 pound chanterelle mushrooms (fresh or dried)
20 almonds
16 pitted black olives
1 celery heart
4 scallions, thinly sliced
1 large tomato
6 large lettuce leaves

Vinaigrette
4 tablespoons walnut oil
3 tablespoons cider vinegar
salt and pepper to taste

1. Clean the mushrooms well. (If you use dried mushrooms, boil them first in 4 cups of water for about 3 minutes and drain.) Cut the ends of the stems off the mushrooms and discard; slice the mushrooms lengthwise into thin pieces. Place them in a deep salad bowl.

2. Slice the almonds and chop the olives; add to the salad bowl. Slice the celery heart and add it to the bowl along with the scallions. Dice the tomato and add it to the bowl.

3. Wash and dry the lettuce leaves. Place one in the center of each of six salad plates.

4. Just before serving, prepare the vinaigrette by mixing all the ingredients well; then pour the dressing over the vegetables. Toss the salad gently and place equal portions of it on top of the lettuce leaves on each of the salad plates. Serve at room temperature.

Portobello Mushroom Risotto

4–6 SERVINGS

3/4 pound fresh or dried portobello mushrooms
4 cups vegetable broth
1/3 cup dry white wine
5 tablespoons olive oil
1 large onion, minced
1 cup uncooked Arborio rice
2 garlic cloves, minced
2 tablespoons fresh thyme (or 1 teapoon dried)
salt and pepper to taste
grated cheese for the table

1. Clean the mushrooms well. Slice them thin and place them in a saucepan. Add the broth and the white wine and bring to a boil. Remove the mushrooms and set them aside, reserving the liquid.

2. Heat the oil in a heavy (cast-iron if possible) saucepan, add the onion and the mushrooms, and stir continuously for $1\frac{1}{2}$ to 2 minutes over medium-low heat.

3. Add the rice, garlic, thyme, and salt and pepper. Stir well. Add $1\frac{1}{4}$ cups of the broth-wine mixture and stir constantly until all the liquid is absorbed. Add another $1\frac{1}{4}$ cups of the broth-wine mixture and repeat the process a third time until all the liquid is absorbed each time.

4. Add the remaining broth-wine mixture and continue stirring at a slower pace until the risotto turns creamy, the rice is tender, and the liquid is absorbed. (The entire process of cooking the risotto should take around 30 minutes.) Serve hot and add a dish of grated cheese at the table for those who wish to add it to their risotto.

Tagliatelle with Mushroom Sauce

1 pound fresh mushrooms
2 tablespoons butter
3 shallots, minced
1 pound tagliatelle
1 (8-ounce) carton heavy cream
4 tablespoons fresh parsley, chopped
salt and pepper to taste

1. Clean the mushrooms. Chop off the stem ends and slice the mushrooms evenly lengthwise.

2. Melt the butter in a deep skillet or saucepan. Add the mushrooms and the shallots. Cover the pan and cook over medium-low heat for about 6 minutes. Stir occasionally.

3. Meanwhile, cook the pasta in boiling salted water for 4–5 minutes, until the tagliatelle is al dente.

4. While the pasta is boiling, add the cream, parsley, and salt and pepper to the mushroom sauce and bring it to a boil. Stir it well. Lower the heat to low and cover the pan so the sauce remains hot.

5. When the tagliatelle is cooked, drain it thoroughly and place it back in its pan. Pour the mushroom sauce over the pasta and mix all the ingredients well. Serve immediately in warm plates, so that the dish remains hot.

MUSHROOMS WITH GARLIC

Serve these mushrooms as an accompaniment to a main course.

4 SERVINGS

$^{1}/_{2}$ pound mushrooms
5 cups water
juice of 1 lemon
6 garlic cloves, minced
4 tablespoons olive oil, plus more if needed
salt and pepper to taste
a few parsley sprigs, finely chopped

1. Clean the mushrooms well. Cut them in slices and discard the stem ends. Place them in a saucepan with the water. Let rest for 15 minutes, then drain thoroughly. Add the lemon juice; mix well.

2. Place the garlic in a deep frying pan. Add the olive oil, mushrooms, and salt and pepper. Cook for a few minutes over medium-low heat. Stir the mixture frequently.

3. When the mushrooms are tender, sprinkle the chopped parsley on top as a garnish.

OKRA

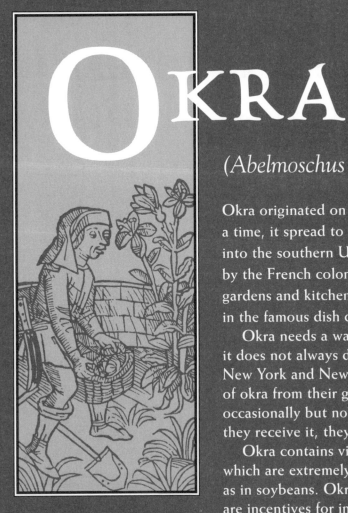

(Abelmoschus esculentus)

Okra originated on the African continent near present-day Ethiopia. After a time, it spread to Arabia and some Asian countries. It was first introduced into the southern United States, in the area of Louisiana and Mississippi, by the French colonists who settled there. It gained prominence in southern gardens and kitchens and has become a staple of Creole cuisine, especially in the famous dish called gumbo (*gumbo* is the Portuguese word for okra).

Okra needs a warm climate for its cultivation, and that is why, perhaps, it does not always do well in the northern states, although I know some New York and New England gardeners who manage to get a good crop of okra from their gardens. In our monastery garden, we cultivate okra occasionally but not every year. Okra plants need a lot of care, and when they receive it, they are prodigious yielders.

Okra contains vitamin A, but its real nutritional value lies in its seeds, which are extremely rich in protein. There is almost as much protein in okra as in soybeans. Okra is also rich in certain minerals and fiber, all of which are incentives for including this vegetable in one's diet, at least from time to time.

SAINT JOSEPH OKRA MEDLEY

This medley, which accompanies meat and egg dishes well, is named after Saint Joseph, the spouse of Mary, and the foster father of Jesus. Saint Joseph, a just and humble man, was always obedient to the Word of God, and thus he is an example of Christian living for all those who follow the monastic path. He is dearly loved by monks and nuns, and he is celebrated with great joy in all monasteries on his feast day, March 19, on May 1, and the Sunday after Christmas.

4–6 SERVINGS

6 tablespoons olive oil
1 large onion, chopped
$^1/_2$ pound okra, cut in 1-inch-thick slices
4 cherry peppers, seeded and sliced
4 garlic cloves, minced
1 celery stalk, sliced
1 cup water or vegetable stock
1 cup dry white wine, plus more if needed
1 bay leaf
8 small new potatoes, peeled and sliced in half
2 teaspoons paprika
2 teaspoons dried thyme
salt and pepper to taste

1. Pour the olive oil into a large skillet. Add the onion, okra, peppers, garlic, and celery and sauté lightly over medium-low heat for 4–5 minutes, until the vegetables are tender. Stir frequently.

2. Add the water or stock, wine, bay leaf, potatoes, paprika, thyme, and salt and pepper. Stir and cover the skillet. Reduce heat to low and simmer gently, stirring from time to time, for 30–40 minutes. Adjust the seasonings as desired and add more wine if liquid is needed. Remove the bay leaf and serve hot.

SCRAMBLED EGGS WITH OKRA

4 SERVINGS

2 tablespoons butter or margarine, plus more if needed
$^1/_3$ pound okra, cut in $^1/_2$-inch slices
1 onion, sliced
1 long bell pepper, sliced
7 eggs
$^1/_2$ cup heavy cream
salt and pepper to taste
4 slices toasted bread

1. Melt the butter in a deep frying pan. Add the okra, onion, and pepper. Sauté over low heat for 3–5 minutes. Add more butter if needed.

2. In a large bowl, beat the eggs well. Add the cream and salt and pepper; mix well. Pour the egg mixture over the vegetables and cook over medium-low heat, stirring often. When the eggs begin to set but are still moist, remove the pan from the heat.

3. Serve the eggs hot on top of toasted bread.

Okra Caponata

4 SERVINGS

1 red onion, sliced
4 garlic cloves, minced
5 tablespoons olive oil
12 okra, sliced
1 large tomato, peeled, seeded, and diced
1 red pepper, diced
$^1/_3$ cup water, plus more if needed
3 tablespoons balsamic vinegar
8 pitted black olives
2 tablespoons drained capers
salt and pepper to taste

1. Sauté the onion and garlic in the olive oil in a cast-iron pot or frying pan until the onion begins to turn golden. Add the okra, tomato, and red pepper. Continue stirring for about 2 minutes.

2. Add the water, vinegar, olives, capers, and salt and pepper. Stir well and cover. Cook over low heat for 10–15 minutes. Stir from time to time and add more water if needed. The caponata is done when most of the liquid has evaporated. Adjust the seasonings as desired and mix well. Remove the pan from the heat and serve warm or cold as an appetizer.

Bill Tarbox's Okra in Tomato Sauce

This dish works well as a side dish to a main course

4–6 SERVINGS

1 pound okra, trimmed and cut in $^1/_2$-inch-thick slices
4 tablespoons olive oil
4 tomatoes, peeled and cut in chunks
1 onion, thinly sliced
salt and pepper to taste
fresh parsley, chopped, as garnish

1. Place the okra in a saucepan and cover sufficiently with water. Bring to a boil and cook for 4–5 minutes. Drain and rinse in cold water.

2. Pour the olive oil into a large skillet or saucepan. Add the tomatoes and onion. Cook over medium-low heat for about 5 minutes, until this turns into a chunky sauce. Add the okra and salt and pepper and continue cooking for 2–3 minutes, stirring continuously.

3. Serve hot with freshly chopped parsley on top.

ONIONS

(Allium cepa)

Like potatoes, onions have universal appeal and are used in culinary concoctions in cultures around the world. A kitchen in which onions are not used is almost unimaginable.

The onion and its many varieties belong to the same species as the lily family. The earliest known species seem to have originated in the western part of Asia, in the region that is today Pakistan and Iran. From Asia, the onion spread to Egypt, where it was held in such esteem that it was considered a sacred fruit, something deserved only by the gods. From Egypt, it was exported to Greece and Rome. While the Greeks seem to have had a certain disdain for the onion, due to its sting and odor, the Romans on the other hand developed a great appreciation and attachment to it. Cultivation of the onion was encouraged and fostered throughout the Roman Empire; the Romans believed that the onion gave extra strength and energy to soldiers on the battlefield.

During the Middle Ages, the onion was given a special honor at the table, where kings and noblemen sang of the magic qualities of the onion and delighted at its inclusion in the most elaborate dishes. As if its culinary qualifications were not enough, the onion was also greatly appreciated for medicinal and therapeutic uses, especially as a laxative.

Today, the onion is recognized as a good source of vitamins B_1 and B_2 and also vitamin C. The green tops of onions, like scallions, should not be thoughtlessly discarded by cooks, for a great deal of the onion's vitamins resides precisely in its green leaves. This is one more reason, for those who can, to cultivate onions in your own garden; you can thus benefit from eating them fresh and whole, green parts included, partaking of all their vitamins.

Garlic, shallots, scallions, chives, and their cousins all belong to the same general family as the onion (*Alliaceae*). These are very useful spices, flavoring agents, and garnishes. They can be used in many varieties of dishes and appear in a number of recipes scattered throughout the book.

ONION TART

This dish is sometimes served as an appetizer, but there is no reason it could not be served as a main course, especially for brunch or dinner.

6 SERVINGS

Pastry Shell (Pâte Brisée)
1 egg
1 cup flour
1 stick butter or margarine
5 tablespoons ice water
pinch salt

Filling
1 pound onions
3 tablespoons butter
2 eggs
1 (8-ounce) carton half-and-half or heavy cream
salt and pepper to taste

1. Prepare the pastry shell by mixing all the ingredients in a deep bowl. Use both a fork and your hands to mix well until the dough comes together. Do not overwork it. Form a ball of dough and sprinkle it with flour. Place the ball in a bowl, cover, and let rest in the refrigerator for 1 hour.

2. While the dough is in the refrigerator, prepare the filling: First, peel and slice the onions. Then melt the butter in a deep skillet, add the onions, and cook over low heat 2–3 minutes, until they turn golden. Stir often with a spatula. Cool for 8–10 minutes and set aside.

3. When the dough is ready to be worked, cover the entire work area with flour and gently roll the dough out, extending it in every direction. Preheat the oven to 250°F. Thoroughly butter a tart pan (or pie pan) and carefully place the rolled dough onto it. (The dough must be handled with the fingers at all times.) Trim the edges in a decorative manner, cover the pastry shell with aluminum foil, and place it in the oven for 10–20 minutes.

4. Increase the oven temperature to 300°F. Beat the eggs in a deep bowl, add the half-and-half or cream and salt and pepper, and continue beating until the mixture is well blended. Add the cooked onions and mix well.

5. Pour the egg-onion mixture into the pastry shell and place it in the oven. Bake for 25–30 minutes. Serve hot.

GLAZED ONIONS

These delicious new onions make a wonderful accompaniment to a main course and are very easy to prepare.

4 SERVINGS

$1/2$ pound small new onions
2 tablespoons butter
2 tablespoons Calvados
pinch salt
pinch granulated sugar

1. Peel the onions carefully so they remain intact. Place them in a deep frying pan and add water to cover their tops. Bring to a boil and cover the pan. Cook for 5 minutes.

2. Turn the heat to low and add the butter, Calvados, salt, and sugar. Mix well and cover. Stir from time to time so the onions are well coated. Allow all the water to evaporate and serve immediately.

ONION SALAD

This is an intriguing and original appetizer and should be served to guests who love onions. Onions cooked this way can also be served as an accompaniment for fish or poultry.

1 pound medium new onions (Vidalia are ideal)
lettuce leaves
sliced tomato (optional)
olives (optional)

Vinaigrette
8 tablespoons olive oil
4 tablespoons raspberry vinegar (or another fruity vinegar)
1 tablespoon mustard
salt and pepper to taste

1. Preheat the oven to 350°F. Place the onions whole and unpeeled in the oven for 30 minutes. Remove and allow them to cool.

2. With a small pointed knife, peel the onions carefully so that they remain intact. When they are all peeled, slice them in half lengthwise.

3. Prepare the vinaigrette by mixing all the ingredients well in a small bowl.

4. On each plate, place two lettuce leaves. Add three or four onion halves on top. Pour the vinaigrette over them and serve. (You could add a couple of tomato slices and a few olives to each serving for extra color.)

Onion Soup Gratinée

6 SERVINGS

6 white onions
2 red onions
$^1/_2$ stick butter or the equivalent in olive oil (about 6 tablespoons)
2 tablespoons cornstarch
6 cups water or stock of your preference
6 tablespoons French brandy
4 bouillon cubes (unless stock is used instead of water— flavor of your choice)
salt and pepper to taste
pinch thyme
6 slices bread
grated Gruyère or other cheese of your preference

1. Peel and slice all the onions. Melt the butter in a soup pot and cook the onions slowly over low heat 2–3 minutes, until they begin to turn brown. Stir continuously.

2. Add the cornstarch. Stir into the onions and mix well. Add the water or stock. Add the brandy and bouillon cubes. Bring to a boil. Boil for 5 minutes, add the salt and pepper and thyme, and turn the heat to low and simmer for 10 more minutes.

3. Meanwhile, preheat the oven to 300°F. Pour the soup into ovenproof soup bowls. Add a slice of bread on top, cover the bread and soup with the grated cheese, and carefully place the bowls in the oven for 5–10 minutes, until all the cheese melts and begins to bubble. Serve immediately.

PEAS

(Pisum sativum)

Recent archaeological studies have shown that peas already existed in 10,000 BC. The pea is perhaps one of the most ancient vegetables known today. Peas are said to have originated in the Orient, in Persia, the area known today as Iran. From there, they gradually traveled to Asia Minor (present-day Turkey), Palestine, and then to Greece and Rome. The humble pea has served many purposes throughout the centuries, including its role in England during the Middle Ages as a form of salary for the poor. Later, it became a fashionable vegetable for the table, especially during the reign of Louis XIV, who was extremely fond of peas.

A great many varieties of peas belong to the same family. Here in the monastery, we cultivate two types: the tender, sweet peas, which can be eaten whole in their shells; and the well-known peas that need to be extracted from their shells prior to being eaten. At the monastery, peas are planted in the garden very early in the season. There is an old monastic tradition of planting the first peas on March 25, the feast of the Annunciation and of Christ's Incarnation. Peas in general do well in cool weather, so planting in early spring creates the wonderful result of being able to harvest fresh peas for the table by early June. Later in the year—in early August, to be precise—we plant peas for the autumn harvest.

Peas are rich in vitamins B, C, and E. They are also rich in protein and carbohydrates, which gives them a high overall nutritional value.

Another variety of pea, one that does not belong to the same family but whose recipes I include here because of their close resemblance, is the chickpea. The chickpea, or *pois chiche* in French, belongs to the *Cicer arietinum* species, and like the pea is a vegetable of great antiquity. It was greatly esteemed by the Romans and thus cultivated in their gardens. The chickpea has remained a favorite of the Mediterranean countries.

Farm-Style Sweet Peas

This is an excellent dish to serve year-round but especially during the late spring or early summer months, when the peas are harvested from the garden.

10 ounces sweet peas, fresh or frozen
12 small onions (cippolina, shallots, or similar)
4 small new carrots
4 tablespoons butter
6 lettuce leaves, finely sliced
1 tablespoon granulated sugar
salt and pepper to taste
fresh parsley, finely chopped, as garnish

1. Remove the peas from their pods (or use frozen ones). Peel the onions and carrots. Slice the carrots into circles.

2. Put the onions and carrots in a saucepan. Add enough water to cover them and bring to a boil. Turn the heat to medium-low and cook for 6–8 minutes.

3. Add the peas, butter, lettuce, sugar, and salt. Mix well and continue cooking for about 10 more minutes. When the vegetables are done, drain and place in a bowl. Adjust the seasonings as desired, add the salt and pepper, and toss the vegetables gently. Sprinkle the chopped parsley on top and serve.

CHICKPEA SALAD

This is a good salad to serve throughout the summer months.

4–6 SERVINGS

2 cups cooked chickpeas, or 2 (15-ounce) cans chickpeas, drained and rinsed
4 carrots, finely grated (in a food processor)
1 medium onion, minced
2 celery stalks, thinly sliced
fresh mint leaves, chopped, (optional)

Dressing
1/3 cup olive oil
4 tablespoons lemon juice
salt and pepper to taste

1. Place the chickpeas in a deep salad bowl. Add the carrots, onion, and celery. Mix well and place the bowl, covered, in the refrigerator for at least 1 hour.

2. Before serving, prepare the salad dressing by mixing all the ingredients well in a small bowl. Pour the dressing into the salad bowl, add the chopped mint if desired, toss the salad gently a few times, and serve immediately.

CREAMY SPLIT PEA SOUP

6 SERVINGS

1 1/2 cups dried split peas
3 carrots, diced
2 leeks, white parts only, sliced
1 onion, sliced
8 cups water, plus more if needed
1 ounce butter
1/2 cup milk (low-fat may be used)
salt and pepper to taste
pinch nutmeg
croutons as garnish

1. Place the peas, carrots, leeks, and onion in a large soup kettle. Add the water and bring to a boil. Turn the heat to medium-low, cover the kettle, and cook for 30 minutes. Remove from the heat and allow it to cool.

2. Blend thoroughly in a blender or food processor in batches. Pour the soup back into the kettle and reheat it. Add the butter, milk, and seasonings, including the nutmeg. Stir the soup several times to mix well. Serve hot, topping each serving with a few croutons.

Snow Peas Chinese Style

4–6 SERVINGS

8 dried Chinese mushrooms (any dried mushrooms can
  be substituted)
$1/2$ pound fresh snow peas
4 tablespoons vegetable oil
1 (4-ounce) can bamboo shoots, drained and sliced
salt to taste
1½ tablespoons soy sauce
1 teaspoon granulated sugar
1 bunch chives, finely chopped, as garnish

1. Soak the mushrooms in warm water for $1/4$ hour.
Slice evenly and discard the stems.

2. Wash the snow peas; trim the ends and strings.
Place in a saucepan with water to generously cover.
Bring to a boil, cover the pot, and turn off the heat.
Let the snow peas rest for 10 minutes; drain them.

3. Pour 2 tablespoons of oil into a wok or deep
frying pan. Heat to medium and let the oil get hot.
Add the snow peas and stir continuously for 30–40
seconds. Remove the peas and set aside.

4. Pour the remaining 2 tablespoons of oil into the
wok or frying pan; add the mushrooms, bamboo
shoots, salt, soy sauce, and sugar. Cook for 1–2
minutes, stirring constantly. Add the snow peas, mix
well, and serve hot. Garnish with chives.

PEPPERS

(Capsicum annuum)

There are endless varieties of peppers around the world. Some are from Asia and India, but the majority originated here, on the vast American continent, and were said to be discovered by Christopher Columbus in the region known today as Central America. Columbus, according to the writer Pierre Marty, discovered the pepper during his first trip to the Americas. He then took it with him back to Spain to show the Spaniards the sort of fruit-vegetable that formed part of the diet of the indigenous peoples here. The type of pepper that Columbus imported to Europe was hot and spicy, probably some sort of the so-called chili pepper. It immediately was adopted by the Spaniards as a new source of spice for their dishes and given the name *pimento* in Spanish (*piment* or *poivron* in French). From there, the pepper has become, across all cultures, the product most used to spice a dish. What would we do without ground black pepper? The same could be said of cayenne, paprika, and white pepper. There is no doubt that pepper has become the most universal of all spices, helping to enhance dishes from the simple to the complex.

The large peppers are said to be originally from Brazil, and from there their cultivation was extended to Portugal and other regions of the world. These peppers, which are very popular in our supermarkets, can be green, yellow, or red. There is also the long, light green sweet bell pepper, very popular in Italy, where it is often fried. The sweet bell pepper has been increasing in popularity in American gardens and at the table. In our monastery garden it is one of the few types of peppers cultivated annually; others include the large, dark green pepper and some of the small spicy ones, which I often use in pickling and for flavoring certain dips and other dishes.

Peppers are rich in vitamins A, B, B_2, and E. They are also used as color sources for many dishes. In certain regions those fighting rheumatism are encouraged to eat peppers. Peppers in general are low in calories, but their nutritional value diminishes when they are cooked.

RED PEPPER LIGHT SAUCE

You can substitute 1 1/2 cups heavy cream for the light white sauce if you wish. Heat the heavy cream to boiling, add the red pepper sauce and some freshly ground pepper, and mix well. This makes a lighter, smoother sauce, or coulis.

6–8 SERVINGS

4 sweet red peppers
6 tablespoons olive oil, plus more as needed
fresh parsley, chopped (optional)

Light White Sauce
2 tablespoons cornstarch
1 1/2 cups milk
2 tablespoons butter
salt and pepper to taste
dash nutmeg

1. Cut each pepper into quarters and remove the seeds. Place the peppers in an ovenproof dish under the broiler until they begin to burn or char. Remove them from the oven, allow them to cool, and then peel.

2. Place the peeled peppers in a food processor, add the olive oil, and blend thoroughly until the mixture turns into a smooth sauce. Add chopped parsley if desired, for a bit of extra flavor.

3. Prepare the light white sauce by dissolving the cornstarch in the milk in a small bowl. Then melt the butter in a saucepan. When the butter begins foaming, add the milk-cornstarch mixture and stir assiduously. Add the salt and pepper and nutmeg. Continue to stir until the sauce is smooth and thick.

4. Add the red pepper sauce to the white sauce and mix thoroughly. Serve hot over fish, vegetables, meats, plain rice, or an omelet.

RED PEPPER AND MESCLUN SALAD

This is an elegant appetizer at any time of the year.

6–8 SERVINGS

4 large red peppers
1 medium white onion, thinly sliced
1¹/2 pounds mesclun, washed, trimmed, and drained
1 small radicchio, sliced into strips lengthwise
8 ounces mozzarella cheese, thinly sliced, as garnish

Vinaigrette
¹/4 cup olive oil
3 tablespoons wine vinegar
salt and pepper to taste

1. Preheat the oven to 350°F and bake or broil the peppers for about 20 minutes, turning them from time to time. When they are blackened, allow them to cool in a closed paper bag. Then peel and open them, remove the seeds, and slice lengthwise into strips.

2. Place the peppers in a deep salad bowl. Add the onion, mesclun, and radicchio and mix well.

3. Just before serving, prepare the vinaigrette by mixing all of the ingredients in a small bowl. Pour the dressing over the salad and toss gently. Serve on individual plates and top each serving with slices of mozzarella cheese.

Yellow and Red Pepper Salad

This is an excellent dish to serve as an appetizer for a dinner or even lunch or brunch.

6–8 SERVINGS

2 large yellow peppers, cored and seeded
2 large red peppers, cored and seeded
1 pound green beans (haricots verts—the thinner, the better)
1 red onion, thinly sliced
finely chopped fresh parsley

Vinaigrette
$1/2$ cup olive oil
2 tablespoons balsamic vinegar
1 teaspoon fresh lemon juice
1 teaspoon Dijon mustard
salt and freshly ground pepper to taste

1. Slice the peppers lengthwise into thin strips and blanch in boiling water for about $1/2$ minute. Drain immediately and run cold water over them to regain their freshness and bright colors. Set aside.

2. Cut the ends off the green beans and trim off any leftover strings. Boil in salted water for 5 minutes; drain and run cold water over them as for the peppers. Set aside.

3. Prepare the vinaigrette by mixing all the ingredients well in a small bowl. When ready to serve, place the vegetables in a salad bowl, pour the vinaigrette over them, and add the parsley. Gently toss the salad until the vegetables and vinaigrette are well mixed. Serve immediately.

Peppers with Tuna Fish

This is an elegant introduction to a good dinner; it can also be served as a Sunday or festive brunch.

4 SERVINGS

2 large red peppers
2 large yellow peppers
6 tablespoons olive oil
4 tablespoons lemon juice
2 garlic cloves, minced
salt and pepper to taste
1 (6-ounce) can tuna fish, drained and crumbled
16 black olives, pitted and chopped
16 capers
fresh basil, finely chopped, as garnish

1. Slice the peppers in perfect halves, lengthwise. Trim the ends and discard the seeds. Place the peppers in a long baking dish and put them under the broiler for 15–20 minutes, until they begin to turn black. Allow them to cool (you may use a paper bag), then peel them, watching carefully that the halves remain intact.

2. Pour the olive oil into a bowl. Add the lemon juice, garlic, and salt and pepper. Mix well, cover the bowl, and place in the refrigerator for at least 45 minutes.

3. When ready to serve, take the bowl from the refrigerator and add the tuna fish, olives, and capers and mix well. Adjust the seasonings as needed.

4. On four individual plates, place half of a roasted red pepper and, beside it, half of a roasted yellow pepper. Place an equal portion of the tuna mixture inside each pepper half. Sprinkle chopped fresh basil over the stuffed peppers and serve.

PEPPERS WITH PASTA

This dish may be served hot or lukewarm but never cold. It is also served without the customary grated cheese on top, although you may sprinkle warm or crumbled goat cheese on each serving.

6 SERVINGS

2 red peppers
2 yellow peppers
2 green peppers
1 onion, peeled
2 garlic cloves, minced
8 tablespoons olive oil
1 pound tagliatelle
small branches fresh marjoram and thyme
salt and pepper to taste
1 (8-ounce) package goat cheese as garnish (optional; see note)

1. Slice the peppers in half and place them with the onion under the broiler for 10–12 minutes, until they are well grilled but not burned. Remove the peppers and onion and allow them to cool.

2. Once they have cooled (you may place them in a paper bag), carefully remove the skin from the peppers and slice them into long, thin pieces, about the same length as the tagliatelle. Carefully slice the onion into long pieces, also. Place the peppers, onion, garlic, and 6 tablespoons of olive oil in an ovenproof bowl. Cover the bowl and keep the mixture warm in the oven at 200°F.

3. Boil the pasta in salted water for 6–7 minutes, watching that it remains al dente. Drain the pasta and place it in a serving bowl. Add the peppers and onion from the oven, the remaining tablespoons of olive oil, the marjoram, thyme, and salt and pepper. Mix well and serve.

POTATOES

(Solanum tuberosum)

If someone were to ask, "Which vegetable is the most popular?" I think most people would respond: the potato. The appeal of the potato seems to be universal. Potatoes are found today in outdoor markets and supermarkets all year round, in nearly every part of the world.

The origins of the potato can be traced to the mountains of the Andes. It was first discovered in Peru by the Spanish conquerors around 1532. The following year, a certain Pedro C. de Leon mentions in his *Peru Chronicles* that potatoes (or *papas*, as they were called by the native Peruvians) and corn were considered essentials in the daily diet of the local Incas. The first potatoes were introduced in Spain around 1533. From Spain, their cultivation extended rapidly to France and Italy. By the beginning of the seventeenth century, the potato was well established in France, where a scientific description of it was offered in the book *Histoire des Plantes*, published in 1601. From France, the cultivation of the potato was extended to Germany, Austria, Switzerland, and other countries to the north. In the eighteenth century, a renewed interest was shown in the potato, thanks to the French pharmacist Antoine A. Parmentier, who spread knowledge of it and its cultivation to every province of France. Parmentier appealed to the king himself, saying that the potato was perhaps the most practical food to grow to feed the king's subjects during times of famine. The appreciation of the potato in France owes so much to Parmentier that even today many potato dishes are called in French by the name *Parmentier*.

Today, more than a hundred varieties of potato are cultivated around the world. I have a farmer friend here in Millbrook, New York, who specializes in potatoes and raises twenty-eight varieties. In our own garden, our needs call for three or four varieties. I particularly appreciate small potatoes, red or otherwise, which enhance many of our dishes.

The potato has a strong nutritional value, as well as being rich in vitamins B_1, B_2, and C. When preparing the potato for cooking, consider the nutritional value of its skin—40 percent of its vitamin C is concentrated there.

Small Potatoes in Yogurt Sauce

6 SERVINGS

$1/3$ cup sesame oil, plus more if needed
$1^1/2$ pounds small potatoes (new, if possible), peeled
1 (16-ounce) container plain yogurt
salt and pepper to taste
1 teaspoon cumin
$1/2$ cup cilantro, finely chopped, plus more as garnish
5 garlic cloves, minced
2 medium onions, chopped

1. Pour the oil into a large skillet or casserole. Add the potatoes whole and sauté gently over medium-low heat for about 5 minutes. Stir frequently and add more oil if needed.

2. Preheat the oven to 350°F. Thoroughly butter a deep ovenproof dish with a lid. Place the potatoes in the dish and add the yogurt, salt and pepper, cumin, $1/2$ cup of the cilantro, garlic, and onions and mix well. Cover the dish and place it in the oven for 50–60 minutes. Then remove and garnish the top with chopped cilantro. Serve hot as an accompaniment to a main course.

Potato and Stilton Cheese Soup

6 SERVINGS

4 medium potatoes, peeled and cubed
2 leeks (white parts only), finely chopped (or 1 medium
    onion, chopped)
3 cups water
3 cups low-fat milk
3 tablespoons butter or margarine
3 tablespoons flour
6 sprigs parsley, minced
salt and white pepper to taste
$1/3$ cup crumbled Stilton cheese

1. In a good-size soup kettle, place the potatoes and the leeks or onion. Pour in the water. Bring to a boil and then reduce the heat to low. Cover the kettle and simmer for about 20 minutes, until the potatoes are tender. Turn off the heat and mash the vegetables with a hand masher.

2. Into a separate saucepan pour the milk and add the butter, flour, parsley, and salt and pepper. Cook over medium heat, stirring continuously, until the milk begins to boil. Then pour the mixture into the kettle containing the potatoes and cook over medium heat until the soup becomes thick and bubbly. Stir frequently. Adjust the seasonings as desired.

3. While the soup is hot and bubbly, add the cheese and stir constantly until it melts and blends well. Serve hot.

Potato Salad Southern French Style

This is an excellent salad to serve during a friendly lunch or brunch.

6–8 SERVINGS

1¹/2 pounds boiling potatoes, peeled and cooked
6 hard-boiled eggs, chopped
6 small tomatoes, cored and quartered
1 small red onion, sliced
¹/2 cup pitted black olives, sliced in half
5 tablespoons capers

Vinaigrette
¹/2 cup olive oil, plus more if needed
4 tablespoons tarragon vinegar, plus more if needed
1 tablespoon Dijon mustard
salt and freshly ground black pepper to taste

1. Dice the potatoes and place them in a good-size salad bowl. Add the eggs, tomatoes, onion, olives, and capers.

2. Prepare the vinaigrette by mixing all the ingredients well in a small bowl. Just before serving, pour the vinaigrette over the vegetables. Toss gently until the vegetables are well coated. Adjust the seasonings as desired and serve.

POTATO CRÊPES À LA PROVENCE

4 SERVINGS

$^1/_2$ cup milk
$^1/_2$ cup beer
3 eggs
3 tablespoons white or whole wheat flour
$^1/_3$ cup fresh parsley, finely chopped
4 garlic cloves, minced
pinch nutmeg
sea salt and freshly ground pepper to taste
2 medium potatoes, peeled and finely grated
4 tablespoons olive oil or butter

1. Combine in a deep bowl the milk, beer, eggs, flour, parsley, garlic, nutmeg, and salt and pepper and whisk together by hand, or in a blender. If the blender is used, pour the mixture back into the bowl. Add the potatoes; mix well.

2. Into a nonstick crêpe pan pour 1 tablespoon of olive oil and turn the heat to medium-high. When the pan gets really hot, pour 1 quarter of the potato batter into it and spread the batter evenly with a spatula to form a crêpe, or pancake. Gently shake the pan a bit over the heat so the crêpe doesn't stick to the bottom. Do this carefully for 2–3 minutes. When the crepe looks solid and cooked at the bottom, carefully turn it over with a spatula and reduce the heat to medium. Cook for 2–3 minutes, until the crêpe is done. Remove it onto a good-size serving plate and keep warm by covering it or placing in a 200°F oven until ready to serve.

3. Repeat the procedure with the remaining batter to make three more crêpes, adding more oil or butter as needed. Serve the crêpes hot as an accompaniment to a main course.

Potato Croquettes Belgian Style

If you are not going to serve the croquettes right away, place them in an ovenproof dish in a 200°F oven to keep them warm. They are a wonderful accompaniment to fish, meat, and egg dishes.

6 SERVINGS

1 pound medium potatoes, peeled and quartered
$^1/_4$ cup flour
3 eggs, separated
4 tablespoons heavy cream
4 tablespoons finely grated cheese (Parmesan or Gruyère)
nutmeg to taste
pinch white pepper
oil or butter for frying

1. Boil the potatoes in salted water to cover. When they are fork tender, drain completely and allow them to dry for at least $^1/_2$ hour in a large, deep bowl.

2. Mash the potatoes thoroughly until they turn almost into a puree but of a rough consistency. Add the flour, well-beaten egg yolks, cream, cheese, nutmeg, and pepper; mix well. Beat the egg whites well in a small bowl and incorporate them gradually into the potato mixture. Place the bowl, covered, in the refrigerator for 1 hour.

3. With your hands, roll a small amount of the potato mixture back and forth on a clean, smooth surface, shaping it into a small ball. Repeat until all the mixture is used up. Place the croquettes in a flat dish so they do not touch.

4. Pour the oil or butter into a frying pan and turn the heat to medium. When the oil or butter is hot, brown the croquettes on all sides a few at a time. This is delicate work. Remove carefully, one at a time, to a serving plate.

Sweet Potatoes with Rum

6 SERVINGS

2 pounds sweet potatoes
3 tablespoons butter
$^1/_2$ cup maple syrup
$^1/_2$ cup orange juice
$^1/_3$ cup raisins
$^1/_2$ tablespoon nutmeg
4 tablespoons rum
pinch salt

1. Boil the sweet potatoes in water to cover for 15–20 minutes. Drain and allow them to cool. Carefully remove the skins.

2. Butter a shallow baking dish. Slice the sweet potatoes lengthwise and carefully place the slices in the dish.

3. Preheat the oven to 350°F. Melt the butter in a saucepan, mix in the remaining ingredients, and sauté over low heat for a few minutes, stirring continuously. Remove the pan from the heat before the mixture starts to boil. Pour mixture evenly over the sweet potato slices. Bake for 30–35 minutes, until the liquid turns into a thick sauce. Serve hot.

New Potatoes with Sage

This dish is good with a fish, egg, or meat main course.

4 SERVINGS

15 medium potatoes, peeled and cut in half
4 tablespoons olive oil
2 onions, sliced
salt to taste
bunch fresh sage leaves
6 garlic cloves
paprika to taste
½ cup water or milk

1. Place the potatoes and water to cover in a large saucepan and bring to a boil. When the potatoes are fork tender, drain and set aside.

2. Pour the oil into a deep skillet and sauté the onions for 2–3 minutes, stirring often. Add the potatoes and sprinkle with salt. Stir again and cook for 2–3 minutes over medium-low heat. Make sure that the potatoes are coated on all sides.

3. Preheat the oven to 350°F. Mince the sage leaves and garlic in a food processor and add them to the potatoes. Add the paprika and continue sautéing and stirring for another 1–2 minutes.

4. Thoroughly butter an ovenproof dish that has a cover. Place the potatoes in it and pour water or milk over them. Cover the pot and place it in the oven for about 30 minutes. Serve the potatoes hot.

Potato Salad Pot-au-Feu

4–6 SERVINGS

8 potatoes, peeled
4 carrots
1 red onion, sliced
8 mushrooms, sliced
fresh parsley, finely chopped, as garnish
black olives, chopped and pitted, as garnish

Vinaigrette
8 tablespoons olive oil
4 tablespoons wine vinegar
1 garlic clove, minced
salt and pepper to taste

1. Boil the potatoes and carrots in water to cover until they are tender; allow them to cool. Cut the potatoes into chunks and slice the carrots. Place them in a salad bowl.

2. Add the onion and mushrooms and toss gently.

3. Prepare the vinaigrette by mixing all the ingredients well in a small bowl. When you are ready to serve, pour the vinaigrette over the vegetables and toss again until they are well coated. Serve on individual plates and top each portion with chopped parsley and olives.

Baked Sweet Potatoes

This is a delightful and appetizing accompaniment to meat, fish, and egg dishes, especially during the fall or winter.

4 SERVINGS

4 large sweet potatoes
$3/4$ cup low-fat sour cream
$1/3$ cup maple syrup
$1/2$ tablespoon dried ginger
$1/2$ tablespoon nutmeg
salt and pepper to taste
butter

1. Preheat the oven to 400°F. Slice each potato carefully in half and bake for 40–50 minutes, until tender. Remove from the oven and lower the temperature to 350°F.

2. With a spoon, carefully scoop out the pulp, keeping the potato skins intact, and put the pulp into a large bowl. Mash the pulp with a masher. Add the sour cream, maple syrup, ginger, nutmeg, and salt and pepper and mix thoroughly.

3. Fill the potato shells with equal amounts of the pulp mixture. Butter a shallow baking dish, put the potatoes in it, and dot each half with a bit of butter. Place in the oven and bake for 25–30 minutes, until they turn brown on the top.

RADISHES

(Raphanus sativus)

Research tells us that the ancient Egyptians cultivated the radish, giving it the name "moon." It was also known to the Mesopotamians and in various regions of the Near East and eventually reached the lands of Greece and Italy. In Greece, it was cultivated for both culinary and medicinal purposes, for the Greeks believed the radish to have curative powers against the cough and hemorrhages.

The radish is a vegetable that most gardeners simply adore. It grows in any type of soil, poor or rich, and it can be harvested for consumption in thirty days! No other vegetable has ever demonstrated such a quick growing record. The secret of having a prolonged harvest, of course, consists in consecutive plantings every two weeks, more or less.

The radish is rich in vitamins B and C but has little other nutritional value. Here in the United States, it is used mainly in salads and hors d'oeuvres; however, I have included some recipes to show that the radish is also excellent as a cooked vegetable. All one needs to do is simply experiment with it.

CANDIED RADISHES

4 SERVINGS

32 radishes
4 teaspoons butter
3 tablespoons granulated sugar
salt and freshly ground pepper to taste
2 tablespoons water
chervil, finely chopped, as garnish

1. Choose fresh, good-looking radishes, more or less of the same size. Wash them well and trim on both sides.

2. Melt the butter in a deep frying pan, add the sugar, salt and pepper, water, and the radishes. Stir a few times, cover the pan, and cook over low heat for 12–15 minutes, or until the water evaporates. Serve hot as an accompaniment to any main dish, topped with chopped chervil.

SAUTÉED RADISHES

4–6 SERVINGS

1 pound large radishes, sliced
3 medium cucumbers, peeled, quartered, and cut into
    1-inch pieces
4 tablespoons white or cider vinegar
4 tablespoons oil or butter
2 tablespoons lemon juice
fresh dill, chopped, as garnish

1. Place the radishes and the cucumbers in a deep bowl. Sprinkle with vinegar and let stand for $1/2$ hour; drain.

2. Pour the oil or melt the butter in a good-size skillet. Add the vegetables and sauté gently for 5–6 minutes over medium-low heat. Don't overcook; they should remain firm and crisp.

3. When the vegetables are done, sprinkle the lemon juice over them. Mix gently, garnish with the chopped dill, and serve warm.

RADISH GREENS PESTO SAUCE

Use this delicious sauce with pasta dishes and with tomatoes and potatoes. It can also be used with fish and eggs. It can be stored in the refrigerator for a long time. If you don't have a food processor, you could make the pesto by hand with a mortar and pestle, adding all the ingredients gradually.

4–6 SERVINGS

2 cups chopped fresh radish greens (the tops)
1 cup chopped fresh basil
1 cup olive oil
6 garlic cloves, minced
$^1/_2$ cup grated Parmesan or Romano cheese
2 tablespoons pine nuts (optional)
salt and freshly ground pepper to taste

1. Place the radish greens and the basil in a food processor. Blend at high speed for a few seconds. Using a spatula, evenly redistribute the greens inside the food processor.

2. Add the olive oil, garlic, cheese, nuts, and salt and pepper and blend at high speed for a few more seconds, until all the ingredients are evenly mixed.

Radish Canapés

This radish-avocado mixture can be prepared ahead of time and kept in the refrigerator until you are ready to use it. Whenever possible, use radishes grown in your own garden. If you do not wish to use bread, you could use your favorite kind of cracker or tortilla.

6–8 PERSONS

20 medium fresh radishes
2 ripe avocados
1 shallot, minced
3 tablespoons olive oil
4 tablespoons fresh lemon juice
salt and pepper to taste
fresh cilantro, finely chopped
6–8 slices bread

1. Trim the radishes at both ends, then cut them in half and slice them thin.

2. Peel the avocados and mash with a fork in a small bowl. Add the shallot, oil, lemon juice, salt and pepper, and chopped cilantro and mix well. Add the radishes and again mix thoroughly until the mixture is smooth.

3. Toast the bread and cut each slice in four equal pieces. Spread the radish-avocado mixture on each toast square and serve as an appetizer.

Salad Greens

In early summer, a variety of salad greens begin to arrive in our monastery garden. With repeated plantings throughout the season, we are happy to enjoy the freshness and delight that these greens bring to the table for a long time. All the cook has to do is use his or her imagination to create marvelous concoctions with the diverse variety of tastes, textures, flavors, and nuances of color available. Among the greens cultivated and served at the monastic table are the following:

Lettuce (*Lactuca sativa*) is perhaps the best known and the most cultivated of the salad greens. Already known in antiquity, it was considered a sacred vegetable by the ancient Egyptians. They used it in ritual ceremonies as a form of offering and homage to the goddess of fertility, for they strongly believed that lettuce possessed aphrodisiac-like qualities. The Greeks and the Romans found other virtues and medicinal qualities in lettuce. For instance, they considered it a great help in sleeping and strongly recommended its consumption by insomniacs.

Today there are hundreds and hundreds of varieties of lettuce available for home cultivation in the garden. There is also a great variety available at the supermarkets. Thank God, gone by are the days when iceberg was the only type of lettuce found in the supermarkets of America. Among the favorites in our gardens are Bibb, Boston lettuce, romaine, Batavia, and those whose seeds we bring from France: Lollo Rossa and Merveille des Quatre Saisons.

This type of chicory (*Cichorium intybus*), sometimes called endive in the supermarkets (but not to be confused with Belgian endive, p. 111) has a bit of a bitter flavor, and when mixed with other greens in a salad bowl, it creates a marvelous contrast. Our favorite type is called in French *chicorée frisée*. Among this type of frisée, the one that renders excellent results for us is the Grosse pancalière, whose seeds we obtain from France, although they can probably also be found here. One of the many attributes of the frisée, besides its exquisite taste and texture, is its insensitivity to heat and cold. It lingers in the garden long after the first frost but is sensitive to heat.

The arugula (*Eruca vesicaria*) is sometimes called rocket, from the French *roquette*. It originated in the Mediterranean countries of Europe, where it is still widely cultivated and greatly appreciated in salads. Its peppery flavor blends harmoniously with some of the milder greens in the salad bowl. We cultivate two or three types of arugula in our garden: the annual, which is the one most available in American gardens; then a French type called roquette cultivée; and we are particularly fond of the arugula selvatica, a perennial. The seeds from this last one were brought to us from Venice, Italy, by a dear friend who visited there. It has remained a perennial in our garden, where it grows so profusely that each year we have to discard some of its many plants, for it tends to take over the garden. Friends and neighbors have benefited from it, and now it has become abundant in their gardens, as well.

We also cultivate other salad greens in our garden—escarole, mâche, mesclun, mustard greens, and radishes—with wonderful results for the salad bowl because they complement each other. I am quite fond of watercress, use it frequently in salads and soups, and have included it in a few recipes here; unfortunately, we don't have the necessary conditions for its cultivation on our property (it grows well by streams, as its name tells us, and we have none on the monastery land).

ESCAROLE SALAD WITH HARD-BOILED EGGS

This delicious salad can be served as an appetizer or as a separate dish after a main course. It is particularly appetizing during the summer months, when you can harvest the vegetables from your own garden.

6 SERVINGS

1 head tender escarole
1 red onion, thinly sliced
6 hard-boiled eggs, sliced in half, lengthwise
24 cherry tomatoes, sliced in half

Vinaigrette
8 tablespoons virgin olive oil
1 tablespoon lemon juice
3 tablespoons balsamic vinegar
salt and freshly ground pepper to taste

1. Wash the escarole well. Choose the best and most tender leaves from the center and discard the tougher, outer ones. Drain the leaves thoroughly and mix them with the onion. Distribute the escarole and onion mixture evenly among six serving plates.

2. Evenly distribute the eggs and tomatoes on the top of the escarole in a decorative fashion.

3. Prepare the vinaigrette by mixing all the ingredients well in a small bowl. Pour the dressing over each salad just before serving.

Boston Lettuce Mimosa Salad

This is an easy and excellent salad to serve year-round.

4 SERVINGS

1 medium head Boston lettuce
1 medium cucumber, peeled and sliced
1 medium onion, sliced
2 hard-boiled eggs, finely chopped, as garnish

Vinaigrette
6 tablespoons olive oil
3 tablespoons balsamic vinegar
1 teaspoon mustard
salt and pepper to taste

1. Wash the lettuce thoroughly; drain. Separate the individual leaves and place them in a bowl. Add the cucumber and onion.

2. Prepare the vinaigrette by mixing all the ingredients well in a small bowl. When you are ready to serve, pour the vinaigrette over the salad and toss lightly.

3. Serve the salad on four individual plates and sprinkle the chopped eggs over each serving.

Arugula Gourmet Salad

4–6 SERVINGS

1 large bunch fresh arugula, trimmed
1 head radicchio, sliced lengthwise in half
2 Belgian endives, sliced lengthwise in half
1 small bunch watercress, stems trimmed
1/2 pound mâche

Vinaigrette
1/3 cup olive oil
3 tablespoons balsamic vinegar or good red wine vinegar
salt and freshly ground pepper to taste

1. Place the salad ingredients in a large salad bowl.

2. Prepare the vinaigrette by mixing all the ingredients well in a small bowl.

3. Just before serving, pour the vinaigrette over the greens and toss until all the greens are well coated. Serve immediately.

Romaine Lettuce Salad alla Romana

This dish is a wonderful introduction to a good meal—lunch, brunch, or supper.

6 SERVINGS

1 head romaine lettuce, washed, dried, and cut into bite-size pieces
6 medium tomatoes, quartered
1 red onion, sliced into thin rings
1 cup green olives, pitted
2 cups cubed fresh mozzarella, as garnish

Vinaigrette
8 tablespoons olive oil, plus more if needed
2 tablespoons red wine vinegar, plus more if needed
2 tablespoons lemon juice, plus more if needed
salt and black pepper to taste

1. Distribute the lettuce evenly among six salad plates.

2. Place the tomatoes, onion, and olives in a deep bowl. Toss gently; then distribute them evenly over the beds of lettuce. Garnish each serving with the mozzarella.

3. When you are ready to serve, mix all the vinaigrette ingredients well in a small bowl. Pour over each salad. Serve immediately.

CREAMY WATERCRESS SOUP

This is a delicious and elegant first course for a good dinner.

4 SERVINGS

3 large potatoes, peeled and sliced
2 leeks, sliced (white part only)
1 large bunch watercress, chopped
7 cups water, plus more if needed
3 tablespoons butter
1 cup heavy cream, half-and-half, whole milk, or
    low-fat milk
salt and freshly ground pepper to taste

1. Place the potatoes, leeks, and watercress in a large saucepan. Add the water and bring to a boil. Cover the pot and simmer the soup gently for 30 minutes. Set the saucepan aside and allow to cool.

2. When the soup has cooled, blend it in small batches in the blender.

3. Melt the butter in the saucepan and add the batches of blended soup as they come out of the blender. Add the cream and salt and pepper; stir well. Over medium-low heat, bring it to a light boil. Stir again and cover the pan. Serve the soup hot or refrigerate for a few hours and serve cold.

Basic Mâche Salad

4 SERVINGS

1 large bunch mâche
2 Belgian endives
1 small onion
2 apples
fresh parsley or chives, finely chopped, as garnish (optional)

Dressing
$1/2$ cup low-fat plain yogurt or sour cream
1 tablespoon Crème Fraîche
2 tablespoons olive oil
2 tablespoons fresh lemon juice
1 teaspoon creamy mustard (without seeds)
salt and pepper to taste

1. Wash and dry the mâche and endives. Peel the onion and the apples, slice, and place in a large salad bowl with the greens; mix gently.

2. Prepare the dressing by mixing all the ingredients well in a separate bowl. Beat steadily until the mixture turns into a consistently creamy dressing. Refrigerate until you are ready to use.

3. Just before serving, pour the dressing over the salad. Toss the salad, garnish with chopped parsley or chives, and serve immediately.

Summer Mesclun Salad Provençal Style

4 SERVINGS

1 pound fresh mesclun
$^{1}/_{3}$ cup fresh cilantro, chopped
$^{1}/_{3}$ cup fresh chervil, chopped
$^{1}/_{3}$ cup fresh chives, chopped
$^{1}/_{3}$ cup fresh parsley, chopped
3 tablespoons apricot or raspberry vinegar
3 tablespoons olive oil
1 teaspoon honey
sea salt and freshly ground pepper to taste
1 teaspoon Dijon mustard
crumbled goat cheese, as garnish (optional)

1. Wash the mesclun and the herbs and dry thoroughly; toss together in a large bowl.

2. In a good-size bowl combine the vinegar, olive oil, honey, and salt and pepper, and mustard. Whisk the vinaigrette until it is well mixed.

3. Just before serving, pour the vinaigrette over the salad greens and toss gently. If you are using goat cheese, crumble it in the center of the salad as garnish. Serve immediately, either as an appetizer or after a main course.

Arugula Pesto Sauce

Use this sauce for pasta dishes and with tomatoes and zucchini. It can also be used to stuff hard-boiled eggs.

MAKES 1¾ CUP

6 garlic cloves, minced
1 large bunch arugula, chopped
¹/₃ cup pine nuts, well-chopped
6 teaspoons grated Romano (or Parmesan) cheese
1 cup olive oil
pinch salt and pepper

Place all the ingredients in a food processor or blender and mix thoroughly for a few minutes, until everything is well blended.

Romaine Lettuce Salad with Gorgonzola

This is an easy salad to prepare, and it can be served year-round.

6–8 SERVINGS

1 head romaine lettuce, cut into 3-inch sections
1 small head radicchio, thinly sliced
1 red onion, thinly sliced
1 small cucumber, peeled and thinly sliced

Dressing
1 (8-ounce) container sour cream (low-fat is fine)
3/4 cup crumbled Gorgonzola
2 tablespoons olive oil
4 tablespoons fresh lemon juice
salt and pepper to taste

1. Place the vegetables in a good-size salad bowl.

2. In a separate bowl, mix the sour cream, cheese, olive oil, lemon juice, and salt and pepper. Beat by hand until all the ingredients are well mixed and turn into a creamy dressing.

3. Just before serving, pour the dressing over the vegetables and gently toss the salad. Serve immediately.

BASIC ARUGULA SALAD

This salad is ideal for serving after the main course and before dessert.

4–6 SERVINGS

1 large bunch arugula, trimmed
1 small head radicchio, sliced
1 small cucumber, peeled and thinly sliced
1 small onion, sliced
crumbled blue cheese (or goat cheese), as garnish

Vinaigrette
6 tablespoons olive oil
3 tablespoons tarragon-scented vinegar
salt and pepper to taste

1. Place the arugula, radicchio, cucumber, and onion in a good-size bowl.

2. When you are ready to serve, prepare the vinaigrette by mixing all the ingredients well. Pour the vinaigrette over the vegetables. Toss the salad lightly until it is well coated with the vinaigrette. Serve on individual plates and place some cheese on top of each serving as garnish.

ROMAINE LETTUCE SOUP

6 SERVINGS

1 head romaine lettuce, sliced
2 leeks, including the green parts, sliced
3 medium potatoes, peeled and diced
8$^{1}/_{2}$ cups water
2 garlic cloves, minced
salt and pepper to taste
1 (8-ounce) container heavy cream
croutons as garnish (for hot soup)

1. Place the vegetables in a soup pot. Add the water and the garlic and bring to a boil. Reduce the heat to medium-low and continue cooking for another 20–25 minutes. Remove from the heat and let cool.

2. Whirl the soup in a food processor or blender. Return it to the soup pot and reheat over low heat, adding the salt and pepper and the cream, and stir continuously until all ingredients are mixed. This soup can be served hot or cold. If served hot, add some croutons to each serving as garnish.

SPINACH, SWISS CHARD & SORREL

These three green leaf vegetables are usually (or often, in the case of spinach) eaten cooked, in contrast to the green leaf vegetables in the previous chapter, which are eaten raw, usually in salads.

Spinach (*Spinacia oleracea*) has gone through different periods of evolution and change throughout the centuries. The original plant seems to have been Spinacia letandra, which grew wild throughout Asia Minor. From there, spinach was imported to Europe and other parts of the world, undergoing some changes in the process of adaptation to new territories and forms of cultivation. The Europeans first discovered spinach in the Middle Ages, around the time of the Crusades, and were happy to bring home the first seeds for cultivation. Later on, during the time of the Arab invasions of southern Europe, spinach saw further expansion of its cultivation throughout the continents. It is claimed by some that the original Arabic name for spinach was esbanach, which was then latinized as spinacia in Europe. During the eleventh century, Spain's city of Seville became one of the great centers of its cultivation, for spinach was used not only for culinary purposes but also for medicinal ones. During the Renaissance, Catherine de Médicis and her Italian culinary entourage did much to enhance the value of spinach at the table in Paris and throughout France.

Spinach is rich in vitamins A, B, and C, as well as iron and other minerals. That is why it has appropriately become appropriately so integral a part of the twentieth-century diet almost everywhere on the globe. Its cultivation in the garden is relatively easy except that it does not like extremely hot temperatures. For that reason, in our monastery garden, it is usually cultivated in early spring and again in late summer for a fall harvest. One of the great pleasures of late spring and early summer is the arrival of new tender spinach at the monastic table for the first time each year.

Swiss chard (*Beta vulgaris cicla*) plays an integral part in all Latin Mediterranean cooking. Italy, France, and Spain are probably where the largest concentration of cultivation of Swiss chard takes place worldwide.

The origins of Swiss chard seem to have been the borders of both the Mediterranean Sea and the Atlantic Ocean. Chard was appreciated by the ancient Greeks and Romans, especially the poor people of those days, who often used it in soups and other dishes. Swiss chard and beets belong to the same species (*Beta vulgaris*), the difference being that the beet develops an edible root. The greens of both plants are excellent when cooked, and they often substitute for spinach at the monastery table, especially during the height of summer, when our spinach plants go to seed. I have always had a certain preference for Swiss chard, which probably has to do with childhood memories; Swiss chard was frequently used at home and was often preferred to spinach. I usually cook the green leaves as I would spinach and save the stems and cook them separately. There are different types of chards for garden cultivation. We plant two or three different varieties in the monastery garden: regular Swiss chard, available just about everywhere in this country; the poirée blonde, whose seeds we bring from France and which produces a much larger sort of chard; and, last but not least, in some years, the red type of chard, which is both edible and ornamental in the garden. One of the great qualities of Swiss chard is its resistance to both heat and cold. It does well during the heat of summer and tends to endure the first frosts, surviving well into late fall and early winter.

Although not yet as well known in the United States as it is in Europe, sorrel (*Rumex acetosa*) is beginning to receive more recognition among American gardeners and chefs. Perhaps the day will come soon when it will be easy to find in the supermarkets. Those who have it in their gardens do not have to worry about it, for sorrel is a perennial that returns every year. Early in the spring, when I long for something fresh from the garden, I always make recourse to the one thing that is available at that time: sorrel. Unfailingly, it is there before anything else, and one can prepare wonderful soups and delightful sauces with it.

Swiss Chard and Egg Noodles

6–8 SERVINGS

1 pound Swiss chard
1 (12-ounce) package egg noodles
pinch salt
6 garlic cloves, peeled
12 fresh basil leaves
4 sprigs fresh Italian parsley
10 tablespoons olive oil, or to taste
salt and pepper to taste
grated Parmesan cheese

1. Wash and dry the chard, remove the stems, and chop the leaves. (The stems can be used separately for another dish; see Swiss Chard Mont-Voiron, page 208.) Place the leaves in a large saucepan with water to cover and bring to a boil. Reduce the heat to medium-low and cook for 8–10 minutes. Drain the chard and set it aside.

2. In a separate saucepan, cook the noodles according to the instructions on the package; add a pinch of salt. Drain the noodles when they are cooked.

3. While the Swiss chard and the noodles are cooking, place the garlic cloves, basil, and parsley in a food processor or blender and whirl several times until they are finely chopped.

4. Heat the olive oil in a large, heavy pan and add the garlic and herbs. Stir continuously for about $^{1}/_{2}$ minute. Add the Swiss chard, noodles, and salt and pepper and continue stirring until all the ingredients are well mixed. Serve hot and sprinkle grated cheese on top.

SPINACH WITH CROUTONS

4–6 SERVINGS

2 pounds fresh spinach, washed and trimmed
$1/2$ cup heavy cream or half-and-half
3 hard-boiled eggs, chopped, as garnish

Béchamel Sauce
2 tablespoons butter
1 tablespoon cornstarch
1 cup milk
1 tablespoon dry vermouth
salt and pepper to taste
a pinch of nutmeg

Croutons
6 slices bread
6 tablespoons olive oil
2 garlic cloves, minced
a pinch of dried thyme

1. Cook the spinach in salted boiling water for about 5–6 minutes. Drain it and run cold water over it to help retain the fresh color. Drain thoroughly for a second time; chop and set aside.

2. Prepare the béchamel by melting the butter in a stainless-steel pot over medium-low heat. Add the cornstarch and stir continuously with a wooden spoon. Add the milk little by little, stirring continuously. Add the vermouth, salt and pepper, and nutmeg. When the sauce begins to boil, reduce the heat and continue cooking and stirring until it thickens; set aside.

3. Prepare the croutons by cutting the bread into cubes. Pour the olive oil into a wide skillet; add the garlic, bread cubes, and thyme; mix well. Sauté over low heat for 3–5 minutes, stirring continuously. When the cubes are browned on all sides, remove from the heat and set aside.

4. Preheat the oven to 300°F. Thoroughly butter a long ovenproof dish and place in it the cooked spinach, béchamel, heavy cream, and croutons. Mix well and distribute evenly throughout the dish. Place the dish in the oven for 20–25 minutes. Serve hot and garnish each serving with a spoonful or two of hard-boiled egg.

Spinach-Stuffed Apples

8 SERVINGS

8 large apples
juice of 1 lemon
$^1/_4$ pound spinach, fresh or frozen
1 small onion
3 tablespoons, plus 4 teaspoons butter
1 (1$^1/_2$-ounce box) raisins
salt and pepper to taste

1. Using a thin knife and a teaspoon, carefully core and scoop out the inside of each apple, making sure the shape remains intact.

2. Cut the scooped-out part of the apples into small pieces and pour the lemon juice over them; mix well.

3. Cut the spinach and onion into thin, small pieces. Melt 3 tablespoons of butter in a frying pan. Add the spinach, onion, raisins, and apple pieces; sauté for 10 minutes; stirring frequently. Add salt and pepper and mix well.

4. Preheat the oven to 350°F. Fill the apple shells with the stuffing and put $^1/_2$ teaspoon of butter on top of each. Place them in the oven for 20 minutes. Serve hot.

Spinach Chiffonade

4–6 SERVINGS

12 porcini mushrooms (or 6–8 portobello mushrooms), dried
6 tablespoons olive oil
1 pound fresh spinach (young, if possible)
4 teaspoons butter
4 tablespoons lemon juice
salt and pepper to taste

Shallot Sauce
2 shallots, finely chopped
1 cup dry white wine
5 teaspoons butter
10 tablespoons water
salt and freshly ground pepper
lemon juice

1. To prepare the mushrooms, soak them in water for $1/2$ hour, then rinse carefully, so that any sand or dirt is removed. Chop coarsely. Pour about 5 tablespoons olive oil into a large frying pan and sauté the mushrooms over medium heat for 2–3 minutes, until they become tender. Remove from the heat and set them aside.

2. Rinse the spinach and drain. Pour the remaining 1 tablespoon of oil into a large saucepan; add the butter, spinach, lemon juice, and salt and pepper and cook the spinach over medium heat for 4–5 minutes, just until it wilts, stirring constantly. Remove from the heat.

3. Place the lightly cooked spinach in a good-size, well-buttered, ovenproof dish. Spread the cooked mushrooms evenly over the spinach. Cover the dish with a lid or aluminium foil and place it in the oven at 150°F while preparing the Shallot Sauce.

4. To make the shallot sauce, place the shallots in a small pan and add $1/2$ cup of wine. Cook over medium-low heat, stirring continuously, until the wine is almost completely evaporated. Add the butter, water, the remaining $1/2$ cup wine, and salt and pepper and continue cooking and stirring for about 3 minutes.

5. Remove the spinach dish from the oven and increase the temperature to 300°F. Spread the Shallot Sauce evenly over the whole dish and sprinkle some extra lemon juice on the top. Cover the dish again and place it in the oven for 20–25 minutes. Serve hot.

SPINACH TERRINE

Swiss chard can be substituted for the spinach.

4 SERVINGS

1 pound fresh spinach
1 onion, chopped
2 tablespoons butter

Béchamel Sauce
2 tablespoons butter
2 tablespoons cornstarch
2 cups milk
pinch nutmeg
salt and pepper to taste
4 eggs

1. Wash and drain the spinach; chop it coarsely. Boil for 2 minutes in salted water; drain thoroughly and set aside.

2. Sauté the chopped onion in the butter until it begins to turn golden. Remove it from the heat and mix with the spinach.

3. To prepare the béchamel sauce, melt the butter in a saucepan over medium-low heat, then add the cornstarch and stir continuously with a whisk or wooden spoon. Add the milk gradually, whisking or stirring continuously. Add the nutmeg and salt and pepper and continue stirring. When the sauce begins to boil, reduce the heat and continue cooking slowly until it thickens. Remove it from the heat and set aside.

4. Preheat the oven to 350°F. In a large, deep bowl beat the eggs well, add the béchamel sauce, and mix. Add the spinach-onion mixture and mix all the ingredients thoroughly.

5. Butter a bread pan or mold well. Pour the spinach mixture into it. Place the pan in the oven inside a long, flat baking dish filled with water halfway up the sides of the bread pan. (This dish is cooked in what is called a *bain-marie*, or water bath.) Cook for 30 minutes and then allow the terrine to cool a bit before unmolding it. This dish can be served hot or cold.

SORREL SAUCE

This sauce can be served over white fish, white rice, noodles, or hard-boiled eggs.

MAKES ABOUT 1½ CUPS

¹/2 pound sorrel
¹/2 cup vegetable, fish, or chicken stock
1¹/2 tablespoons butter
1 tablespoon cornstarch
¹/3 cup heavy cream
salt and pepper to taste
pinch nutmeg

1. Wash, dry, and trim the sorrel. Discard the stalk in the middle and chop the leaves.

2. Bring the stock to a boil, add the sorrel, and simmer for 6–7 minutes. Set the sorrel aside for a few minutes, allowing it to cool, then put it through a blender.

3. Melt the butter in a saucepan, add the cornstarch, and stir continuously until it is evenly blended. Add the sorrel and continue cooking over low heat for 3–4 minutes, stirring constantly. Add the cream, salt and pepper, and nutmeg and continue stirring for 1–2 minutes, until the sauce is perfectly blended.

Swiss Chard Mont-Voiron

4 SERVINGS

20 Swiss chard stalks
salt to taste
$^1/_2$ stick butter
juice of 1 lemon
2 garlic cloves, minced
6 tablespoons grated cheese (such as Parmesan or
   provolone)
2 eggs, beaten
salt and pepper to taste

1. Separate the leaves of the chard from the stalks.
(Keep the greens to use in another dish; see Swiss
Chard and Egg Noodles, page 201.) Slice the
stalks approximately 3 inches long. Place them in
a saucepan with boiling water. Add salt and cook
for 5–6 minutes maximum; drain well.

2. Melt the butter in a large, heavy skillet. Add the
chard stalks, lemon juice, and garlic and cook over
medium-low heat for about 3 minutes; stirring
frequently. Add the grated cheese and continue
stirring for about 2 minutes, until the ingredients
are well mixed.

3. Just before serving, beat the eggs and add salt
and pepper in a small bowl. Add the eggs to the
chard-cheese mixture. Mix until the eggs are cooked
and well blended with the other ingredients. Serve
immediately.

COLD SORREL SOUP

4–6 SERVINGS

1 large bunch sorrel leaves
1 large leek, white part only
3 tablespoons butter
6 cups water
1 vegetable bouillon cube
1 large cucumber, peeled, seeded, and sliced
1 (8-ounce) container half-and-half
4 tablespoons lemon juice
salt and pepper to taste
6 thin slices smoked salmon, as garnish

1. Trim and chop the sorrel and discard the stems. Thoroughly wash the leek and then slice.

2. Melt the butter in a soup pot; add the sorrel and leek and cook over medium-low heat for about 2 minutes, until the vegetables are wilted and begin to change color. Add the water and the bouillon cube. Bring to a boil, cover the pot, and cook for 5 minutes. Remove from the heat and let cool.

3. Place the cucumber slices and half-and-half in a blender and whirl it for a minute. Add the sorrel soup, lemon juice, and salt and pepper and whirl until all the ingredients are thoroughly mixed and creamy. (This can be done in stages, depending on the amount of the soup.) Refrigerate for a few hours.

4. Just before serving, slice the salmon in long, thin slices julienne style. Serve the soup cold and top it with the salmon.

SORREL OMELET

This is a very popular omelet in France and an attractive dish to serve for a Sunday brunch among close friends.

6 tablespoons butter
1 bunch sorrel leaves, trimmed, stemmed, and chopped
1 (8-ounce) container heavy cream
6 eggs
salt and pepper to taste
chervil, finely chopped, as garnish

1. Melt 3 tablespoons of the butter in a large skillet, add the chopped sorrel, and cook for 2–3 minutes, until the sorrel is thoroughly wilted. Place it in a bowl and add half of the cream; mix well.

2. Beat the eggs in a bowl, counting at least twenty brisk strokes. Add the remaining cream and salt and pepper and continue beating the mixture until well blended.

3. Melt the 3 remaining tablespoons of butter in the skillet; run it all over the pan and let it get bubbly hot, but do not let it burn. Pour in the egg mixture quickly before the butter begins to turn brown. Spread the mixture evenly around the skillet with the help of a spatula. When the egg mixture sets firmly on the bottom, turn the omelet by placing a large dish over it and turning the pan upside down quickly. Gently slide the omelet back into the skillet and pour the sorrel mixture over it. Cover the skillet and allow the omelet to cook for about 2 minutes.

4. Fold one half of the omelet carefully over the other half. Remove it from the pan and slice it into two or three portions. Serve immediately on warm plates with chopped chervil on top of each portion.

SQUASH

(Cucurbita)

The squash is a fruit of tropical origin widely cultivated as a vegetable. Traces of evidence have been found showing that it was already being cultivated in Peru and the Andean countries surrounding it 1,200 years BC. There are many species of squash, or "cucurbits," that belong to the same family. The most renowned today is the pumpkin, or *potiron* in French, but there are also other commonly used varieties, such as butternut squash, acorn squash, yellow squash, Hubbard squash, and gourds. The melon also belongs to this family—it is simply another variety.

The squash is a rustic, basic plant that usually does not need much care except for a good amount of sun and water. It grows in almost any type of soil, though best results are achieved with a soil rich in compost and of sufficient depth. We usually wait to plant our squash at least until mid-May. Here in the northeastern United States, we always have to deal with the fact that all it takes is an unseasonably cold night to kill the young, tender plants or seedlings. Most members of the squash family are not cold resistant—all to the contrary!

We grow different varieties of squash in our small monastic garden and use them not only to serve at the table but also to make jams, preserves, and chutney. The squash is a resilient fruit-vegetable that if kept under the right conditions—in the cellar, for example—can last a long time and thus be a source of culinary delights during the long winter months.

I still have vivid recollections of the old monastic traditions of France. During the time of the harvest, the monks and nuns lined up the squash and pumpkins of all sizes and colors along the cloister corridor for the winter months, and the cook would fetch the ones he needed. I was always amused to see the monks marching in daily processions through a cloister corridor lined with pumpkins. There was a certain resemblance between the line of pumpkins in perfect order and the line of monks in procession.

FESTIVE PUMPKIN SOUP

This is a delightful soup to serve when pumpkins and squash are in season.

6–8 SERVINGS

1 medium pumpkin, peeled and diced
6 potatoes, peeled and diced
2 leeks, sliced (white parts only)
1 onion, diced
2 garlic cloves, minced
1 celery stalk, finely sliced
12 cups water
salt and pepper to taste
1 egg yolk
$^1/_2$ cup heavy cream
grated Gruyère cheese for the table

1. Place the vegetables in a large soup pot. Add the water and bring to a boil. Lower the heat to medium, add the salt and pepper, and cook for about 45 minutes without covering the pot.

2. When the soup is done, allow it to cool and then whirl it in the blender (in batches if necessary). Reheat the soup gradually.

3. Beat the egg yolk in a bowl, add the cream, and continue beating until well mixed. Pour mixture into the soup and stir for 1–2 minutes, until all elements are perfectly blended. Serve the soup hot accompanied by a bowl of grated Gruyère at the table.

PUMPKIN SQUASH au GRATIN

This dish is a good accompaniment to a main course.

4–6 SERVINGS
4 pounds fresh pumpkin
1^1/$_2$ cups split orange lentils
1 pint half-and-half
1 cup thinly sliced low-fat mozzarella cheese
freshly ground pepper to taste
^{1}/$_2$ teaspoon nutmeg
finely grated cheese to taste (such as Gruyère)

1. Peel the pumpkin and slice it into cubes (8–10 cups). Combine the pumpkin and the lentils in a large saucepan and cover with salted water. Bring to a boil, then reduce the heat and continue cooking for 12–15 minutes, until the lentils are well cooked.

2. Drain the vegetables and place them back in the empty saucepan. Add the half-and-half, mozzarella, salt and pepper, and nutmeg. Mix thoroughly and mash the mixture with a masher until it turns into a smooth puree.

3. Preheat the oven to 350°F. Thoroughly butter a long, flat, ovenproof dish and pour the vegetable mixture into it. With a spatula, spread the mixture evenly. Sprinkle grated cheese on top.

4. Place the dish in the oven for about 20 minutes. Serve hot.

ACORN SQUASH SOUP

4–6 SERVINGS

6 tablespoons olive oil
2 onions, chopped
8 cups water or vegetable or chicken stock
3 acorn squash, peeled, halved, seeded, and cut into chunks
1 potato, peeled and cubed
2 carrots, sliced
^{1}/$_2$ cup fresh parsley, minced
salt and pepper to taste
pinch nutmeg
fresh parsley, chopped, as garnish

1. Pour the olive oil into a good-size saucepan and sauté the onions over low heat for about 3 minutes. Turn off the heat, add the water or stock, cover the pan, and let the flavor of the onions permeate the liquid for 15 minutes.

2. Add the squash, potato, and carrots. Stir well and bring to a boil. Reduce the heat, add the parsley and seasonings, cover the pot, and allow the soup to simmer for 30–40 minutes. Add more water if necessary.

3. Allow the soup to cool and whirl it in a blender in small batches. Return the pureed soup to a clean pot. Reheat it over low heat, stir well, and serve hot. Garnish with chopped parsley.

Acorn Squash Stuffed with Goat Cheese

4 SERVINGS

2 medium acorn squash
6 to 8 cups water
4 tablespoons olive oil
1 onion, chopped
2 large tomatoes, finely chopped
2 garlic cloves, minced
handful of fresh parsley, finely chopped
fresh rosemary leaves, if possible
fresh basil leaves, finely chopped
1 (8-ounce package) goat cheese
4 tablespoons bread crumbs
salt and pepper to taste

1. Slice the squash in half and remove the seeds. Add salted water to a large saucepan, and bring to a boil. Place the squash halves in the pan, cut side down, and boil for 8–10 minutes. Drain thoroughly.

2. Heat the oil in a large skillet and add the onion, tomatoes, garlic, and herbs. Sauté for 2–3 minutes, until the mixture turns into a sauce. Remove from the heat and pour into a bowl.

3. Crumble the goat cheese and add it to the sauce. Add the bread crumbs and salt and pepper, and mix well.

4. Preheat the oven to 300°F. Butter a shallow baking dish and arrange the squash halves in it, cut side up. Divide the sauce mixture evenly among the squash halves, filling the cavities to the top. Bake for 30 minutes. Serve hot.

TOMATOES

(Lycopersicon esculentum)

The tomato, properly speaking, is not a vegetable but a fruit. Its origin lies in the ancient mountains of Peru, the Andes. The early Spaniards who discovered and settled in that part of the Americas made acquaintance with the tomato there and later introduced it to Europe. The Spaniards found that the native Indians used the tomato to make a very spicy sauce, which is the origin of our tomato sauce and salsa, so popular today.

The tomato, as well as the potato, also recently discovered, began to be cultivated in Europe, especially in Italy, where it received the name *pomodore*, or "golden apple." From Italy and Spain, it was introduced to France, where the French began calling it *pomme d'amour*, or "love apple," because they believed it to have strong aphrodisiac qualities.

Today the tomato has gained acceptance everywhere and is cultivated worldwide. It may be one of the most popularly consumed fruits, especially among those fruits regularly eaten as vegetables. There are endless varieties for cultivation, from those that mature early to those that arrive later in the season and are excellent for canning for winter use. Tomatoes love the sun, and those that arrive in August or early September usually taste better, for they have been saturated by the heat from the sun. Tomatoes are rich in vitamins A, B, and C, as well as iron and magnesium. The one part of the tomato that people sometimes find difficult to digest is the skin, in which case it is better to peel it before eating. In the monastery we spend a great part of September and October making tomato sauce and canning it for the winter ahead. I usually boil the tomatoes whole for about 2 minutes and then peel them before turning them into a sauce. Boiling first makes the peeling simpler and faster.

TOMATO VELOUTÉ

4–6 SERVINGS

4 tablespoons olive oil
1 pound tomatoes, peeled and seeded
3 carrots, sliced
2 onions, sliced
1 potato, peeled and sliced
1 (8-ounce) can tomato sauce
a few sprigs fresh parsley, finely chopped
$1/4$ teaspoon dried thyme
salt and freshly ground pepper to taste
8 cups water
$1/2$ (8-ounce container) crème fraîche or low-fat yogurt

1. Pour the oil into a large saucepan and add the tomatoes, carrots, onions, potato, tomato sauce, parsley, thyme, and salt and pepper. Sauté gently over low heat for about 3 minutes, stirring continuously.

2. Add the water and stir well. Bring to a boil and cover the pot. Cook for $1/2$ hour over medium-low heat. Stir from time to time.

3. When the soup is done, set it aside and allow it to cool; then whirl it in batches in a blender. If it will be served cold, place it in the refrigerator. If it will be served hot, reheat it before serving but do not let it boil again. In either case, just before serving, add the crème fraîche or yogurt and mix the soup well.

Tomato and Mozzarella Salad

Serve this dish as an appetizer at lunch or supper.

4 red tomatoes
2 yellow tomatoes
1 red onion, thinly sliced and separated into rings
12 fresh basil leaves, or more according to taste
$1/2$ pound fresh mozzarella cheese, sliced
olive oil to taste
balsamic vinegar to taste
salt and freshly ground pepper to taste
8 black olives as garnish

1. Slice the tomatoes evenly. Distribute the slices on four serving plates.

2. Next to the tomato slices on each plate, place an equal amount of onion rings, basil leaves, and mozzarella slices.

3. Just before serving, lightly sprinkle the olive oil, vinegar, and salt and pepper over each serving. Add black olives to each plate.

TOMATILLO GREEN SAUCE
(Salsa Verde)

The sauce can be used immediately, frozen for later use, or canned in small sterilized jars for future use. It is excellent with Mexican or southwestern dishes.

ABOUT 4 CUPS

1 pound tomatillos, sliced in halves or quarters
2 medium onions, chopped
3 garlic cloves
2 green bell peppers, seeded and chopped
1 small green chili pepper, fresh, canned, or pickled
1/2 cup fresh cilantro, chopped
1/2 cup plus 3 tablespoons olive oil
2 tablespoons lime juice
1 cup water
1½ teaspoons salt

1. Combine all the ingredients except the 3 tablespoons olive oil in a blender or food processor and blend until it becomes a smooth sauce.

2. Pour the 3 tablespoons of olive oil into a deep, heavy skillet or saucepan. Pour the tomatillo sauce into it and simmer over low heat, stirring continuously for 10–15 minutes. Set sauce aside and allow it to cool.

TOMATILLO DIP

Serve the dip with tortilla or corn chips.

2 CUPS

1 cup Tomatillo Green Sauce
1 cup sour cream

Mix the sauce with the sour cream in a small bowl. Blend thoroughly by hand. Place the dip in the refrigerator until you are ready to use it.

TOMATO SALAD ALSATIAN STYLE

This appetizing salad can be served as the main course of a brunch or lunch or as an appetizer before a main course.

6 SERVINGS

6 tomatoes, quartered
6 small potatoes, peeled, boiled, and quartered
1 large Bermuda onion, finely chopped
5 hard-boiled eggs, quartered
$1/2$ cup fresh parsley, finely chopped
green olives, pitted and halved, as garnish

Vinaigrette
7 tablespoons olive oil
3 tablespoons white vinegar
salt and freshly ground pepper to taste

1. Place the vegetables and the eggs in a deep bowl and add the parsley.

2. Mix all the ingredients for the vinaigrette in a small bowl. Pour the dressing over the salad and toss gently a few times.

3. When ready to serve, distribute the salad evenly among six plates. Add a few sliced olives on top of each serving.

TOMATOES À LA JOINVILLE

This dish can be served as the main course of a light lunch during the summer months or as an attractive appetizer for dinner.

6 SERVINGS

6 medium tomatoes
pinch salt
2 tablespoons lemon juice
40 shrimp, thinly sliced
$^1/_2$ cup mayonnaise
pinch cayenne pepper (optional)
12 black olives, pitted, as garnish
lettuce leaves for serving

1. Cut each tomato into two even pieces. With a thin knife and small spoon, scoop out the insides of the tomatoes with care, keeping the shells intact. Place the tomato pulp in a blender and whirl it three or four times. Place the tomato puree in a large bowl.

2. Fill a large pot with water, enough to cover the shrimp. Add salt and lemon juice to the water and bring to a boil. Add the shrimp and cook them until they turn pink, about 5 minutes. Drain the shrimp and place them in the refrigerator for $^1/_2$ hour, or until you are ready to use them.

3. Just before serving, add the shrimp, mayonnaise, and cayenne pepper to the tomato puree and mix everything well. (Refrigerate if not used immediately.)

4. Spread two or three lettuce leaves and two tomato shells on each serving plate. Fill each tomato shell with the shrimp mixture, place an olive in the center of each, and serve.

Tomatoes Stuffed with Goat Cheese

This is a delicious dish to serve as an appetizer or even as a main course. If it is served as an appetizer, serve on top of lettuce leaves. If it is served as a main course, add some plain white rice cooked with herbs on the side.

4 SERVINGS

4 medium tomatoes
10 ounces goat cheese
4 tablespoons olive oil
pinch dried thyme
pinch dried rosemary
salt and pepper to taste

1. Preheat the oven to 300°F. Slice off the tops of the tomatoes and with great care hollow out their insides, keeping the shells intact. Place the tomato shells upside down on a paper towel for at least 10–15 minutes to get rid of any remaining juice.

2. Preheat the oven to 300°F. In a deep bowl, mix the goat cheese, oil, thyme, rosemary, and salt and pepper. Mix well with a fork. Fill each tomato shell with one-quarter of the goat cheese mixture.

3. Place the stuffed tomatoes in a well-buttered, shallow baking dish. Bake the tomatoes for about 20 minutes.

TOMATOES PROVENÇAL STYLE

8 SERVINGS

8 medium to large firm tomatoes
8 tablespoons olive oil
1 onion, finely chopped
4 garlic cloves, minced
4 tablespoons fresh parsley, finely chopped
4 tablespoons fresh basil, finely chopped
1 teaspoon fresh thyme, minced
1 teaspoon fresh rosemary, crumbled
1 egg
$^1/_3$ cup milk
1 cup bread crumbs
salt and pepper to taste
grated cheese, preferably Gruyère (optional)

1. Cut off and discard the tops of the tomatoes, just a little below the stem, and scoop out the pulp with a small spoon, being careful to keep the shells intact.

2. Heat the oil in a large skillet, then add the tomato pulp, onion, garlic, and herbs. Sauté for a few minutes until it all blends well.

3. Preheat the oven to 350°F. In a deep bowl, beat the egg with the milk. Add the contents of the skillet, bread crumbs, and salt and pepper. Mix very well and fill the tomato shells with this mixture. Sprinkle the top with grated cheese, if desired. Butter a shallow baking dish and carefully place the tomatoes in it. Bake for about 30 minutes. Serve hot.

TURNIPS

(Brassica napus)

The origin of the turnip is unknown, although there is evidence that it was already in use during prehistoric times. Both the Romans and the Greeks held this humble root vegetable in high esteem. During the Middle Ages, the turnip, together with the cabbage, was probably the most popular vegetable in Europe. Once America was discovered, it also began to appear in the New World under the influence of English, Spanish, and French colonists, who had a certain predilection for the turnip.

Today turnips come in all sizes, colors, and shapes. Here in the monastic garden, we are provided with excellent seeds from France and cultivate several varieties. First of all, we cultivate a small white turnip that is very tender and a great delicacy in many of our home dishes. Then there is the yellow turnip from France, which is wonderful in soup and pureed dishes. There is also the well-known white turnip with a bit of purple on the top, which is easy to grow and appears in most supermarkets. One type of turnip we don't grow in our garden and seldom used at our table is the rutabaga (*Brassica napus napobrassica*), which belongs to a different category of the turnip family.

Turnips contain a great deal of water and some sugar. They also contain vitamins A and B. It is unfortunate that this humble vegetable is not taken more seriously by cooks and gardeners. In ancient times, it was used as a remedy for many illnesses, especially those of pulmonary origin, such as asthma. It was also said to be of salutary influence on the stomach. I think it is about time to rediscover the culinary value of the turnip and make more frequent use of it at the table.

TURNIPS COUNTRY STYLE

Turnips prepared this way are a good accompaniment to a main course and can take the place of the frequently used potato.

4–6 SERVINGS

8 medium firm white turnips
5 tablespoons walnut oil
salt and pepper to taste
chervil, finely chopped, or crumbled bacon, as garnish

1. Wash the turnips well and trim at both ends. Cut into 1-inch-thick round slices.

2. Place the turnip slices in a saucepan with salted water to cover, and bring to a quick boil. Boil the turnips for 1 minute and drain immediately, pouring cold water over them. Set aside and allow them to dry.

3. Heat the oil in a deep frying pan over medium-low heat and add the turnip slices. Stir them with a spatula and allow them to brown on both sides. Add salt and pepper. Serve immediately, garnished with chervil or bacon.

Turnips and Carrots in Maple Syrup

4 SERVINGS

6 medium white turnips, cubed
3 carrots, sliced in rounds
4 tablespoons butter
1 tablespoon dried mustard
1 tablespoon brown sugar
4 tablespoons maple syrup
pinch ginger
salt and freshly ground pepper to taste
1 (1^1/$_2$-ounce box) raisins (optional)

1. Bring salted water to a boil in a good-size saucepan. Add the turnips and carrots and boil for 6–7 minutes. Drain immediately and set aside.

2. Melt the butter in a large, deep skillet over medium-low heat. Add the mustard, brown sugar, maple syrup, and ginger, mixing very well. Reduce the heat to low and add the turnips and carrots, salt and pepper, and raisins if desired. Stir often until the vegetables are well coated with the maple syrup sauce.

3. Preheat the oven to 300°F and thoroughly butter a sufficiently deep ovenproof dish. Place the vegetables neatly in the dish, covering with a lid or aluminum foil. Bake for 25–30 minutes. Serve the vegetables hot, as an accompaniment to a main course.

TURNIP TIMBALES

6 SERVINGS

9 medium white turnips, peeled and cubed
2 tablespoons butter
3 eggs
1 (8-ounce container) half-and-half
salt and white pepper to taste
1/4 teaspoon nutmeg
fresh chervil or parsley, finely chopped, as garnish

1. Bring water to a boil in a large saucepan and add the turnips. Cook for 30 minutes. Drain and then process them in a food processor in batches until they turn into a puree of even consistency.

2. Melt the butter in the saucepan and add the pureed turnips. Continue cooking them over low heat for a few minutes, stirring continuously so the bottom does not burn. After 3–4 minutes, remove the pan from the stove and let the turnips cool.

3. Break the eggs into a blender and add the half-and-half and seasonings. Whirl in the blender until thoroughly mixed. Gradually pour the egg mixture into the pureed turnips, whisking with the other hand to blend as you go; mix well.

4. Preheat the oven to 350°F and thoroughly butter six small ramekins. Divide the turnip mixture among the ramekins.

5. Carefully put the ramekins into a long roasting pan and add water to the roasting pan up to half the height of the ramekins. Bake for about 45 minutes, until firm and smooth. Add more water to the roasting pan during the cooking if necessary, so that the pan is never dry.

6. When the timbales are done, remove from the water bath and allow them to cool for a minute before unmolding them. To unmold them, go around the edges of the timbales with a small thin knife. Do this slowly and with great care; then place a small plate on top of the ramekin and quickly turn it upside down. Lift the ramekin off with care so the timbale remains intact. The timbales can be served hot or cold, garnished with chervil.

Zucchini & Yellow Squash

(*Cucurbitaceae pepo*)

The zucchini and the yellow squash belong to the cucurbitaceae family, as do all the squash. They are treated separately here because I consider them to be summertime vegetables. The rest of the squash can appropriately be called winter vegetables, since they are generally harvested at the end of the growing season when winter begins.

The zucchini squash seems to have originated in India, where it has been cultivated for many centuries. Zucchini and yellow squash do well in warm-weather climates, as do other types of squash. This is one reason we never plant it before the beginning of May. Sometimes, if the spring is cooler than usual, we will even wait until after the middle of May to sow the first seeds. In the monastery garden, we usually grow three types of this summer squash: the so-called yellow squash; the Cocozella zucchini, coucourzelle in French; and the Ronde de Nice, which is a round type of zucchini, cultivated throughout Provence, from where we import the seeds. This last type of squash we usually bake. It has more flavor than the other zucchini, and when stuffed with day-old bread and Provençal herbs it becomes a true culinary delight.

The zucchini has achieved great popularity in Italy and France, as well as throughout the United States. One of its qualities is its versatility, for it lends itself to many uses, from the popular zucchini bread to baked zucchini and zucchini soups. It harmonizes well with other vegetables and other ingredients, and it demands very little time for cooking, which makes it an ideal vegetable to prepare when one is pressed for time.

ZUCCHINI COMPOTE WITH CORIANDER

4 SERVINGS

8 small zucchini
2 onions
6 tablespoons olive oil
juice of 1 lemon
15 coriander seeds
1 cup water
salt and pepper to taste
fresh mint leaves, finely chopped, as garnish

1. Slice the zucchini (not too thin) and mince the onions.

2. Pour the olive oil into a fairly deep skillet. Add the zucchini, onions, lemon juice, coriander seeds, water, and salt and pepper. Cover the pot and cook over medium-low heat for 15–20 minutes. Make sure the vegetables don't overcook. Stir gently from time to time.

3. Garnish the compote with the mint and serve warm or cold as an accompaniment to eggs, fish, meat, beans, lentils, or rice.

ZUCCHINI MONEGASQUE STYLE

Yellow squash can be substituted for the zucchini in this dish.

4–6 SERVINGS

6 medium zucchini
6 tomatoes, boiled, peeled, and sliced
1 onion, sliced
10 basil leaves, chopped
8 tablespoons olive oil
salt and pepper to taste
1 cup grated cheese (such as Parmesan or Gruyère)

1. Slice the zucchini evenly into thin pieces.

2. Sauté the tomatoes, onion, and basil in 3 tablespoons of the olive oil until the mixture becomes a sauce. Season with salt and pepper. When the sauce is done, remove it from the heat.

3. Preheat the oven to 300°F. Grease an ovenproof baking dish with butter or olive oil. Layer the zucchini, grated cheese, and tomato sauce in the baking dish; repeat the layers and cover the top with the remaining 5 tablespoons olive oil.

4. Place the baking dish in the oven for 25–30 minutes. Serve hot as an accompaniment to a main dish.

Basic Zucchini Velouté

4 SERVINGS

2 zucchini
2 leeks
3 tablespoons olive oil
6 cups water
a few mint leaves, chopped
salt and freshly ground pepper to taste
1 (8-ounce container) low-fat sour cream or yogurt

1. Cut the zucchini into thick slices. Slice the white parts of the leeks and discard the green tops.

2. Pour the oil into a soup pot. Add the zucchini and leeks and sauté over medium-low heat for about 3 minutes. Stir frequently.

3. Add the water, about half the mint leaves, and salt and pepper; stir well. Cover the pot, bring to a boil, and reduce the heat to medium-low. Keep the pan covered and let the soup cook gently for 20–25 minutes. Set aside and allow it to cool.

4. Once the soup has cooled, add the sour cream or yogurt. Mix the soup well and then whirl it in small batches in a blender until it reaches a fine, even consistency. Place the soup in the refrigerator for at least 2 hours. Serve cold, adding the rest of the chopped mint leaves on top of each serving.

QUICK YELLOW SQUASH AND PASTA

4 SERVINGS

This is an excellent dish to serve as a main course during the summer months, when the vegetables are available fresh from the garden.

3 medium new yellow squash, sliced (not too thin)
2 cups rotini pasta (or any other of your preference)
2 tablespoons plus 1 cup olive oil
$^3/4$ cup chopped fresh basil
4 garlic cloves, peeled
freshly ground pepper to taste
1 cup cherry tomatoes
grated Parmesan cheese for the table

1. Bring salted water in a large saucepan to a boil. Add the squash, pasta, and 2 tablespoons of olive oil, and cook for 8–10 minutes over medium heat, stirring occasionally. Don't overcook; the pasta should remain al dente.

2. While the squash and pasta are cooking, put the basil and garlic in a food processor and add the remaining cup of olive oil and some pepper. Whirl for about 1 minute, until the sauce acquires a smooth consistency.

3. Slice the cherry tomatoes into halves and set aside.

4. When the squash and pasta are cooked, drain and return to the saucepan. Add the basil sauce and cherry tomatoes and mix with care. Serve immediately accompanied by grated cheese at the table.

STUFFED RONDE DE NICE ZUCCHINI

6 SERVINGS

3 Ronde de Nice zucchini
3 tablespoons olive oil
2 medium onions, chopped
2 garlic cloves, minced
1 tablespoon fresh sage, chopped
1 tablespoon fresh thyme
a few fresh parsley sprigs, chopped
3–4 slices brown bread, crumbled, as needed
2 eggs
$^1/_2$ cup milk
salt and pepper to taste
grated Parmesan or Gruyère cheese as topping

1. Slice the zucchini in half. Scoop out the seeds and leave the rest intact. Place the shells upside down in salted water to just cover them and boil for about 3 minutes. Drain carefully and set aside.

2. Pour the oil into a frying pan, add the onions and all the herbs, including the parsley, and sauté over medium-low heat for about 3 minutes, until the onions begin to turn golden. Add the bread and mix well. Turn off the heat and set aside.

3. Beat the eggs in a deep bowl. Add the milk and salt and pepper and beat some more until well mixed. Add the onion-bread mixture and mix.

4. Preheat the oven to 300°F. Thoroughly butter a long Pyrex or other ovenproof dish and carefully place the zucchini shells in it. Fill each shell with the onion-egg mixture. Cover each top with grated cheese. Place the dish in the oven and bake for 30 minutes. Serve hot.

YELLOW AND ZUCCHINI SQUASH WITH WINE

This dish is a good accompaniment for grains such as rice, millet, couscous, and lentils. It also goes well with fish and poultry.

6–8 SERVINGS

3 yellow squash
3 zucchini, chopped julienne style
6 tablespoons olive oil
2 medium onions, sliced
1 cup dry white wine, plus more if necessary
2 garlic cloves, minced
2 tablespoons lemon juice
fresh basil, chopped, to taste
fresh parsley, chopped, to taste
salt and pepper to taste
grated Parmesan cheese as garnish

1. Chop the yellow squash and zucchini julienne in sticks as for french fries. If they are very large, discard the seeds.

2. Pour the olive oil into a large, deep skillet, add the onions, and sauté them over medium-low heat for about 2 minutes; stir continuously. Add the squash and continue sautéing for another 2 minutes while continuing to stir. Add the wine and toss gently. Cover the skillet, reduce the heat to low, and cook for 5–6 minutes, until the wine begins to evaporate.

3. Add the garlic, lemon juice, herbs, and salt and pepper. Toss gently for a few seconds until well mixed and then remove the skillet from the heat. Serve the squash hot and sprinkle grated Parmesan cheese on top.

PRESERVATION & CANNING OF VEGETABLES

(with Selected Recipes)

Canning of fruits and vegetables follows these steps:

1. Preparation: Make sure the rims of the glass jars are not cracked or chipped. The metal lids must have a complete ring of sealant; ideally, each lid is used only once and then discarded.

2. Sterilization: Jars and tops must be cleaned by being placed in boiling water for 20 minutes or more.

3. Filling: After the jars are removed from the water (with tongs or another instrument) and drained, loosely fill the jars with vegetables and the liquid in which they were boiled to between $1/2$ and 1 inch from the top. (See "Some Tips on Choosing and Preparing Vegetables," page 243.)

4. Sealing: Poke a nonmetallic utensil into the materials to dislodge any air bubbles. Clean the jar rim and top and cover with a lid. Screw on the sealing band, making sure it fits tightly.

5. Processing: Use a pressure canner to complete the sterilization of the canned vegetables. Follow the instructions for your pressure canner to ensure properly processed food. Then allow the canned food to cool. (Some food products—tomatoes, pickles, jellies, and sauces—do not require a pressure canner. They can be boiled in a large pot with the cans completely immersed in water. Before placing the jars in the water, put a rack on the bottom of the pot to prevent the glass containers from touching the bottom. Do not overpack the pot with jars; allow enough room for water to circulate between the jars. Boil for 30–40 minutes for sauces, 80 minutes for whole vegetables, such as tomatoes.)

6. Verification: Once the filled jars have been sterilized, check for a proper seal—the lid should be slightly curved inward. If the seal has not been made, the lid can be tightened and the sterilization process repeated.

Note: It is important that sterilization and processing are done for an adequate length of time to make sure that all microorganisms are killed and a proper seal is achieved.

YELLOW SQUASH–ZUCCHINI RELISH

ABOUT 2 PINTS

1 cup yellow squash, chopped
1 cup zucchini, chopped
1 onion, chopped
1 green bell pepper, chopped
1 red bell pepper, chopped
2 tablespoons salt
1³/4 cups granulated sugar
1 cup cider vinegar
2 teaspoons celery seed
1 teaspoon mustard seed

1. Combine the squash, zucchini, onion, and green and red peppers. Shake salt over all and cover with cold water. Let stand for 2 hours; drain, pressing the vegetables to remove as much moisture as possible.

2. In another pot, bring the rest of the ingredients to a boil. Add the vegetables and simmer for 10 minutes.

3. Pack the hot mixture into hot, sterilized jars, up to ¹/2 inch from the top. Put the lids on the jars and seal them by placing the jars in boiling water to completely cover them. Boil for at least 15 minutes. Remove the jars from the water bath and allow them to cool. Make sure the tops are thoroughly sealed.

Basic Monastery Salsa

ABOUT 6 PINTS

10 cups peeled, cored, and chopped tomatoes
5 bell peppers, chopped
5 cups chopped onions
1 jalapeño pepper, seeded and chopped
1 1/4 cups cider vinegar
4 cloves garlic, minced
4 tablespoons fresh cilantro, minced
3 tablespoons fresh parsley, minced
3 teaspoons salt
1/2 teaspoon hot pepper

1. Place all ingredients in a large saucepan. Bring to a boil and then reduce the heat to simmer for 20 minutes.

2. Pack the hot mixture into hot, sterilized jars, up to 1/2 inch from the top. Put the lids on the jars and seal them by placing the jars in boiling water to completely cover them. Boil for at least 15 minutes. Remove the jars from the water bath and allow them to cool. Make sure the tops are thoroughly sealed.

Provençal Tomato Sauce

ABOUT 7 PINTS

20 tomatoes, peeled, cored, and chopped
2 celery stalks, sliced
2 carrots, sliced
1 large onion, chopped
3 garlic cloves, minced
12 fresh basil leaves
1 bay leaf
salt and pepper to taste

1. Combine all ingredients in a large saucepan. Cover and cook at medium-high for 30 minutes, stirring frequently to prevent sticking.

2. Pack the hot mixture into hot, sterilized jars, up to 1/2 inch from the top. Put the lids on the jars and seal them by placing the jars in boiling water to completely cover them. Boil for at least 30 minutes. Remove the jars from the water bath and allow them to cool. Make sure the tops are thoroughly sealed.

Basic Tomato Sauce

ABOUT 7 PINTS

1 large onion, diced
3 garlic cloves, minced
2 tablespoons olive oil
20 tomatoes, peeled, cored, and chopped
1 green bell pepper, diced
1 tablespoon fresh oregano, chopped
10 tablespoons fresh basil, chopped
1 tablespoon fresh rosemary, chopped
1 teaspoon salt
$1/2$ teaspoon pepper

1. Cook the onion and garlic in the oil in a large saucepan until tender. Add all the remaining ingredients and bring to a boil; reduce the heat to low and simmer for 1 hour, stirring occasionally.

2. Process the mixture in batches in a food processor. Then return it to the saucepan and cook over medium-low heat for 1 hour, until it thickens. Stir occasionally to prevent sticking.

3. Pack the hot mixture into hot, sterilized jars, up to $1/2$ inch from the top. Put the lids on the jars and seal them by placing the jars in boiling water to completely cover them. Boil for at least 30 minutes. Remove the jars from the water bath and allow them to cool. Make sure the tops are thoroughly sealed.

MONASTERY CORN RELISH

ABOUT 6 PINTS

18 ears corn
3 medium zucchini, diced
1 large onion, diced
2 green bell peppers, chopped
2 red bell peppers, chopped
1 cup granulated sugar
2 tablespoons dried mustard
1 tablespoon mustard seed
1 tablespoon turmeric
1 tablespoon celery seed
1 tablespoon salt
1 quart white vinegar
1 cup water

1. Place the corn in boiling water for 5 minutes and then cut the kernels from the cob. Place all the ingredients, along with the corn, in a large saucepan. Bring the mixture to a boil; reduce the heat and simmer for 20 minutes.

2. Pack the hot mixture into hot, sterilized jars, up to $1/2$ inch from the top. Put the lids on the jars and seal them by placing the jars in boiling water to completely cover them. Boil for at least 15 minutes. Remove the jars from the water bath and allow them to cool. Make sure the tops are thoroughly sealed.

TUSCAN TOMATO SAUCE

ABOUT 7 PINTS

20 tomatoes, peeled, cored, and chopped
1 celery stalk, sliced
2 zucchini, diced
1 large onion, chopped
1 (8-ounce can) pitted black olives, drained
6 garlic cloves, minced
1 green bell pepper, chopped
2 tablespoons granulated sugar
4 tablespoons olive oil
10 fresh basil leaves
1 bay leaf
salt and pepper to taste

1. Combine all ingredients in a large saucepan. Cover the pan and cook at medium-high for 30 minutes, stirring frequently to prevent sticking.

2. Pack the hot mixture into hot, sterilized jars, up to $1/2$ inch from the top. Put the lids on the jars and seal them by placing the jars in boiling water to completely cover them. Boil for at least 30 minutes. Remove the jars from the water bath and allow them to cool. Make sure the tops are thoroughly sealed.

PEACH-ZUCCHINI CHUTNEY

ABOUT 8 PINTS

20 peaches, peeled, pitted, and chopped
2 medium zucchini, diced
$3/4$ cup raisins
1 large onion, chopped
2 cups brown sugar
1 tablespoon cumin
2 tablespoons dried ginger
$1/4$ cup mustard seed
2 teaspoons salt
2 cloves garlic, minced
1 red pepper, minced
5 cups vinegar

1. Place all ingredients in a large saucepan. Simmer until thick, about 40 minutes. Stir often to avoid sticking.

2. Pack the hot mixture into hot, sterilized jars, up to $1/2$ inch from the top. Put the lids on the jars and seal them by placing the jars in boiling water to completely cover them. Boil for at least 20 minutes. Remove the jars from the water bath and allow them to cool. Make sure the tops are thoroughly sealed.

Cucumber Relish

MAKES ABOUT 6 PINTS

8 cucumbers, diced
5 green bell peppers, finely chopped
3 red bell peppers, finely chopped
4 cloves garlic, minced
1 onion, finely chopped
1 tablespoon turmeric
$^1/_2$ cup salt
2 quarts cold water
1$^1/_2$ cups brown sugar
1 quart white vinegar
1 tablespoon mustard seed
2 teaspoons whole allspice
2 teaspoons whole cloves

1. Combine the cucumbers, peppers, garlic, and onion in a large pot. Sprinkle with the turmeric. In another pot, dissolve the salt in the water and then pour the water over the vegetables. Let stand for 3–4 hours. Drain the vegetables, cover with fresh cold water, and let stand for 1 hour; drain again.

2. Combine the brown sugar and vinegar in a saucepan. Tie the spices in a cheesecloth bag and add to the pan. Bring the mixture to a boil and pour over the vegetables. Cover the pan and let the vegetables stand for 10 hours in a cool place.

3. Return the vegetables to the stove and bring to a boil. Then reduce the heat and simmer until they are heated through.

4. Pack the hot mixture into hot, sterilized jars, up to $^1/_2$ inch from the top. Put the lids on the jars and seal them by placing the jars in boiling water to completely cover them. Boil for at least 20 minutes. Remove the jars from the water bath and allow them to cool. Make sure the tops are thoroughly sealed.

SALTY CUCUMBER PICKLES

ABOUT 3 PINTS

1/3 cup canning salt
2 pounds cucumbers, cut into 1/4-inch-thick slices
2 quarts cold water
4 cups water
5 cups white vinegar
1 cup brown sugar
1 teaspoon celery seed
1 teaspoon mustard seed

1. Pour the salt lightly over the cut cucumbers in a container; add the 2 quarts of cold water and let the cucumbers stand for 2 1/2 hours; drain.

2. In a saucepot, boil 3 cups of water and 3 cups of vinegar. Add the cucumbers, reduce the heat, and simmer for 8 minutes. Remove the cucumbers and set them aside; discard the liquid.

3. Combine the remaining 1 cup of water and 2 cups of vinegar in a saucepot. Add the brown sugar and celery and mustard seeds and bring to a boil. Reduce the heat and simmer for 10 minutes; add the cucumbers. Bring the mixture to a boil again.

4. Pack the hot mixture into hot, sterilized jars, up to 1/2 inch from the top. Put the lids on the jars and seal them by placing the jars in boiling water to completely cover them. Boil for at least 20 minutes. Remove the jars from the water bath and allow them to cool. Make sure the tops are thoroughly sealed.

Apple–Sweet Potato Chutney

This can be made as hot (spicy) as you desire by increasing the sources of spiciness (hot peppers, mustard, and ginger). Alternatively, the dish can be made milder by removing the seeds, a major source of the hot sting, from the hot pepper.

ABOUT 10 PINTS

12 tart apples, peeled, cored, and chopped
4 sweet potatoes, peeled, chopped, cooked, and mashed
2 onions, chopped
2 red bell peppers, diced
2^1/2 cups brown sugar
2 teaspoons cumin
2 teaspoons allspice
3 tablespoons mustard seed
2 tablespoons dried ginger
2 hot red peppers, chopped
2 teaspoons salt
3 garlic cloves, minced
1 quart cider vinegar

1. Place all ingredients in a large saucepan. Simmer until thick, about 1 hour. Stir often to avoid sticking.

2. Pack the hot mixture into hot, sterilized jars, up to ^{1}/2 inch from the top. Put the lids on the jars and seal them by placing the jars in boiling water to completely cover them. Boil for at least 20 minutes. Remove the jars from the water bath and allow them to cool. Make sure the tops are thoroughly sealed.

Some Tips on Choosing & Preparing Vegetables

1. Always choose fresh vegetables and fruits, whether from your own garden, a farmer's stand, or the supermarket. Fresh produce preserves the vital vitamins, nutrients, and fiber needed for your health.

2. Try to obtain and experiment with vegetables that are in season. Use what is most available, which tends to ensure the freshness of the produce. The changing variety of produce throughout the year also seems to suit the varying needs of our bodies. Besides, vegetables that are in season tend to be more economical.

3. When you purchase vegetables, avoid those that look old, damaged, or somehow tarnished. The younger, fresher, and firmer the produce, the more it preserves its original taste, texture, and nutritional value.

4. Whenever possible, ascertain that the vegetables you use are grown organically, free of pesticides. If possible, cultivate your own vegetables in order to avoid any chemical substances, such as pesticides, that can be dangerous to your health. When you are not sure of the provenance of vegetables, clean them thoroughly.

5. It is important to preserve your vegetables properly. Use the refrigerator for those vegetables that need colder temperatures. Some vegetables and fruits, such as potatoes, squash, and apples, can be kept adequately in a cool, dry cellar.

6. If the vegetables you use are from your garden or are organically grown elsewhere, you can use the entire vegetable, including the outer covering. The peel often contains important vitamins and nutrients. However, if you are doubtful about how they have been grown, it may be safer to peel them or scrub them under running water. When using leafy vegetables such as lettuce and cabbage that are not from a garden following natural organic growing methods, remove their outer leaves and trim any areas that could contain residues of pesticides and chemicals.

7. Some vegetables, such as celery root, artichokes, and avocados, tend to oxidize and change color when peeled. Use lemon juice or white vinegar to preserve them from oxidation and to preserve their original color.

8. Do not overcook vegetables. Overcooking tends to diminish the nutritional content as well as the taste and texture of the vegetable. Learn to use the techniques appropriate for each particular vegetable.

9. If you save the water in which your vegetables are cooked or boiled, you can refrigerate it and use it as vegetable bouillon in your next soup. It contains nutrients and is delicious, as well.

10. The presentation of vegetables at the table is important. They should be attractive and appeal visually, as well as by taste and aroma. Besides their nutritional value, vegetables should be chosen on the basis of flavor, shape, color, and texture for as healthy and appetizing a diet as possible.

Vegetables & Their Seasons

Spring

Asparagus
Avocados
Beets
Carrots
Chickpeas
Endive
Jerusalem artichokes
Lentils
Mushrooms
Onions
Peas
Potatoes
Radishes
Salad greens
Spinach
Sorrel
Split peas

Summer

Artichokes
Beans
Beets
Broccoli
Carrots
Cauliflower
Celery
Celery root
Corn
Cucumbers
Eggplant
Okra
Onions
Peppers
Potatoes
Radishes
Salad greens
Tomatoes
Yellow/summer squash
Zucchini

Autumn

Artichokes
Beans
Broccoli
Brussels sprouts
Cabbage
Carrots
Cauliflower
Corn
Cucumbers
Eggplant
Fennel
Leeks
Mâche
Mushrooms
Onions
Peas
Peppers
Potatoes
Pumpkins
Radicchio
Radishes
Salad greens
Sorrel
Spinach
Squash
Sweet potatoes
Swiss chard
Tomatoes
Turnips
Zucchini

Winter

Avocados
Dried beans
Beets
Brussels sprouts
Cabbage
Carrots
Celery
Celery root
Endive
Jerusalem artichokes
Leeks
Lentils
Mushrooms
Onions
Potatoes
Salad greens
Squash
Sweet potatoes
Turnips

INDEX